SpringerBriefs in Law

SpringerBriefs present concise summaries of cutting-edge research and practical applications across a wide spectrum of fields. Featuring compact volumes of 50 to 125 pages, the series covers a range of content from professional to academic. Typical topics might include:

- A timely report of state-of-the art analytical techniques
- A bridge between new research results, as published in journal articles, and a contextual literature review
- A snapshot of a hot or emerging topic
- A presentation of core concepts that students must understand in order to make independent contributions

SpringerBriefs in Law showcase emerging theory, empirical research, and practical application in Law from a global author community. SpringerBriefs are characterized by fast, global electronic dissemination, standard publishing contracts, standardized manuscript preparation and formatting guidelines, and expedited production schedules.

Sara Tommasi

The Risk of Discrimination in the Digital Market

From the Digital Services Act to the Future

Springer

Sara Tommasi
Department of Law Studies
University of Salento
Lecce, Italy

ISSN 2192-855X ISSN 2192-8568 (electronic)
SpringerBriefs in Law
ISBN 978-3-031-43639-0 ISBN 978-3-031-43640-6 (eBook)
https://doi.org/10.1007/978-3-031-43640-6

This Springer imprint is published by the registered company Springer Nature Switzerland AG
The registered company address is: Gewerbestrasse 11, 6330 Cham, Switzerland

Paper in this product is recyclable.

To Maria

Contents

Chapter 1
Introduction

Abstract This chapter starts from the analysis of the Regulation (EU) 2022/2065, known as Digital Services Act, to verify how this new regulation can make a concrete contribution to avoid discrimination within the digital services sector. The EU's attention to discrimination in the digital environment can already be seen in the European Parliament Resolution of 20 October 2020 on the Digital Services Act and fundamental rights issues posed. In this Resolution it is stated that the principle of non-discrimination needs to be ingrained at the core of a successful and durable EU policy on digital services. In contributing to anti-discrimination protection, the Digital Services Act is in line with the European Declaration on Digital Rights and Principles for the Digital Decade, adopted by the Commission on 26 January 2022, in the context of the Digital Decade Policy Programme 2030. The Digital Services Act is complementary to the Regulation (EU) 2022/1925, known as Digital Markets Act. In the Digital Markets Act, non-discrimination is understood as the defence of "contestability", in the digital sector, between the products and services offered by different "business users". The Digital Services Act looks at the risk of discrimination from the point of view of the user of the digital services.

Keywords Digital single market strategy · Digital Decade Policy Programme 2030 · Digital rights · Digital Services Act · Digital Markets Act

1.1 European Union's Digital Single Market Strategy and Digital Services Act

The dependence of our economy and society on digital services is now clear, to such an extent that an exemplification is unnecessary.[1]

[1] On the future of and challenges for European private law, see Janssen et al. (2023), De Franceschi et al. (2019).

S. Tommasi, *The Risk of Discrimination in the Digital Market*,
SpringerBriefs in Law, https://doi.org/10.1007/978-3-031-43640-6_1

However, we are not always sufficiently aware of the potentially discriminatory impact of digital services.[2] Similarly, there is a lack of awareness of the specificity of the online environment, which was born as a space characterised by the absence of intermediation and regulation,[3] and yet so in need of guarantees of security and protection of fundamental rights.[4]

Against this backdrop, it is not surprising that the European Union is committed to drafting a regulation on a single market for digital services. This is Regulation (EU) 2022/2065, known as the Digital Services Act,[5] which together with the Resolutions that preceded it, represents an important milestone in the ambitious construction of a European legal framework for digital services.[6] These are, specifically, the Resolutions of 20 October 2020: one of which is aimed at improving the functioning of the

[2] It is not only necessary to develop projects that guarantee universal access to technologies but also campaigns to raise awareness and education that overcome the possibility of lack of interest, motivation, and knowledge on the part of vulnerable people. This is noted by Pérez-Escolar and Canet (2022), p. 1068. For an interdisciplinary reflection inviting a greater awareness of the vulnerability of the human being, see Turner (2006), Mollo (2021), p. 199. For a reconstruction of the European framework referring to e-accessibility and digital equality, see Rabai (2022), p. 199, Passaglia (2021) p. 1. About the concept of relational vulnerability with special regard to the technological environment, see Gatt and Caggiano (2022) p. 8. The authors highlight the need for a new concept of vulnerability is asserted not related to physiological-cognitive deficits of human beings but to their very condition as humans operating in a digital environment.

[3] On the illusion of "disintermediation" see Lind (2002), p. 150. See Petruso (2002), p. 69, where it is stated that for some time now, one no longer speaks of "disintermediation", but of "reintermediation". On the role of private law in regulating the activities of digital service intermediaries see Wielsch (2019), p. 197, Iannarelli (2022), p. 320. The author states that it is difficult to distinguish between the exclusive relations inherent to civil society and those relating to economic relations in the strict sense of the word, as digitisation implies in all digital relations the presence of the network and its main players.

[4] Camardi (2021), p. 871, recalls the shared and undeniable vocation of the Net to the exaltation of personal freedoms and individual rights, both on the side of the active exercise of people's prerogatives, and as a defence against the new risks and dangers induced by the Net, and therefore a justifying reason for new protection regulations.

[5] Regulation (EU) 2022/2065 on a Single Market for Digital Services and amending Directive 2000/31/EC (hereinafter: Digital Services Act). https://eur-lex.europa.eu. For an analysis of the role of the Digital Services Act in relation to existing EU law, see Busch and Mak (2021), p. 109. Compare Scola (2022), p. 127, Caggiano (2021), p. 139.

[6] A fundamental premise on this point is the Communication from the Commission, known as Shaping Europe's digital future, 19 February 2020. https://ec.europa.eu. There, the Commission's intentions are clear. We read, in fact, that the Commission «wants a European society powered by digital solutions that are strongly rooted in our common values, and that enrich the lives of all of us: people must have the opportunity to develop personally, to choose freely and safely, to engage in society, regardless of their age, gender or professional background. Businesses need a framework that allows them to start up, scale up, pool and use data, to innovate and compete or cooperate on fair terms. And Europe needs to have a choice and pursue the digital transformation in its own way». For a comparison between the European Parliament Resolutions of 20 October 2020 and the previous one European Commission, Communication: Shaping Europe's digital future, 19 February 2020. https://ec.europa.eu compare Moscon (2020), p. 980, Arbia (2020), p. 5.

single market through a reform of e-commerce,[7] the other Resolution focuses on the need for greater fairness, transparency and accountability in the content moderation procedures of digital services.[8]

Fundamental rights issues were the subject of an additional and specific Resolution that notes the need to ensure legal clarity for platforms and users considering the rapid development of technology.[9]

The proposals and contents of these Resolutions are accepted and developed in the Digital Services Act, which does not prejudice, but supplements, the application of the rules of Union law governing certain aspects of the provision of intermediary services.[10]

The Digital Services Act deals both with problems similar to those we were confronted with in 2000, and which were regulated by Directive 2000/31/EC, known as E-Commerce Directive,[11] and with new problems linked to the large audience of online platforms,[12] to the capacity also of algorithms to amplify the diffusion of messages, and to the development of a business model in which some operators, direct the choices of consumers and, in fact, control the access and permanence on the market of companies.[13]

The research that we intend to conduct here starts from the analysis of the Digital Services Act's novelties to verify whether, and how, this new regulation may be able to keep technological innovation going and, at the same time, address the risks it

[7] European Parliament Resolution of 20 October 2020 with recommendations to the Commission on the Digital Services Act: improving the functioning of the Single Market (2020/2018(INL)). https://www.europarl.europa.eu.

[8] European Parliament Resolution of 20 October 2020 with recommendations to the Commission on a Digital Services Act: adapting commercial and civil law rules for commercial entities operating online (2020/2019(INL)). https://www.europarl.europa.eu.

[9] European Parliament Resolution of 20 October 2020 on the Digital Services Act and fundamental rights issues posed (2020/2022(INI)). https://www.europarl.europa.eu.

[10] Adamski (2018), p. 719, analyses the main economic and political benefits, as well as the costs of establishing a European market for online activities and the outcome of the positive integration in this domain before and after the 2015 Digital Single Market Strategy.

[11] Directive 2000/31/EC on certain legal aspects of information society services, in particular electronic commerce, in the internal market. www.eur-lex.europa.eu. The E-Commerce Directive set the ambitious objective for Europe to become the most competitive and dynamic economy in the new environment and to accelerate the uptake of digital technologies across Europe. Compare Schulze and Staudenmayer (2020), Lopez-Tarruella (2001), p. 1337, Ponzanelli (2002), p. 87.

[12] Panetta (2019), p. 1018. For a comparison between the Digital Services Act and E-Commerce Directive, also in terms of platform liability, see Achleitner (2022), p. 114.

[13] On digital firms and the differences with traditional notions of market power, see Mândrescu (2020). On the subject of "business models", albeit with specific reference to Directive (EU) 2019/770 of the European Parliament and of the Council of 20 May 2019 on certain aspects concerning contracts for the supply of digital content and digital services, see Efroni (2020), p. 799. On the "risks of collusion" in the ecosystems created by digital platforms and the fact that the network can increase both consumer surplus and competitive risks in equal measure, see Thomas (2021), p. 53. On the role of platforms "as gateways to consumer information", compare Narciso (2019), p. 557, Van Den Bergh and Weber (2021), p. 29.

entails. Risks that affect the individuals who use digital services, the market and society.[14]

Particular attention will be given to the practical implications of the risk–based approach, which seems to be the thread followed by the European Union in regulating the digital market. The risk approach, from a European perspective, makes it possible not to hinder technological innovation through excessive restrictions, but to govern it with obligations and responsibilities proportionate to the degree of risk introduced by the system.[15] The aim is to create a legal framework that is dynamically adapted to technological evolution and capable of addressing its risks, while respecting fundamental rights and the values of the Union.[16]

Confirmation of the adoption, at European level, of a risk–based approach is also to be found in the Proposal for a Regulation on Artificial Intelligence, of 21 April 2021, hereafter referred to as Artificial Intelligence Act, which is destined to be of global and not just European significance.[17] This can be deduced from Article 2, which defines its scope of application regardless of where the providers are established, but in relation to whether the artificial intelligence systems or the output produced by these systems are used in the Union.[18]

---

[14] One thinks, for example, of organised professional disinformation using the Internet and so-called "active measures", i.e., all those influence activities that are strategically engineered to achieve a certain objective. On these aspects refer to Rid (2022). See also Cornils (2020), p. 25, where it is stated that «with regard to the risks for the news ecosystem arising from platform communication, the phenomena of so-called strategic communication can be distinguished from those of an unintended degeneration of democratic discourse inherent in the functioning and business models of intermediaries—especially social media platforms. While the former is—in principle—little disputed as a disturbing and potentially harming factor and thus, in principle, as a regulatory challenge, the possibility, necessity and legal justifiability of regulatory measures in the latter area are much less clear and more controversial».

[15] See Chamberlain (2023), p. 1, where the critical aspects of the risk approach are also identified. With particular reference to critical risk management profiles, see Iacovelli and Fontana (2022), p. 107.

[16] About the EU legislator's intention to combine the protection of fundamental rights and market interests in the Digital Services Act see Mantelero (2023), p. 107.

[17] Com (2021) 206 final, Proposal for a Regulation of the European Parliament and of the Council laying down harmonised rules on artificial intelligence. (Artificial Intelligence Act) and amending certain union legislative acts. https://eur-lex.europa.eu. See also the Amendments adopted by the European Parliament on 14 June 2023 on the Proposal for a Regulation of the European Parliament and of the Council on laying down harmonised rules on Artificial Intelligence (Artificial Intelligence Act) and amending certain Union legislative acts (COM (2021)0206—C9-0146/2021—2021/0106(COD))1; the Draft Compromise Amendments on the Draft Report Proposal for a Regulation of the European Parliament and of the Council on harmonised rules on Artificial Intelligence (Artificial Intelligence Act) and amending certain Union Legislative Acts, dated 15 May 2023;. Proposal for a Directive on adapting non-contractual civil liability rules to artificial intelligence (Artificial Intelligence Liability Directive), COM (2022) 496 final. https://commission.europa.eu.

[18] See Mökander et al. (2021), p. 2. There it is stated that the importance of the Artificial Intelligence Act and its relevance outside Europe is not only due to the circumstance that it is the «first attempt to elaborate a general legal framework for artificial intelligence carried out by any major global economy», but also because multinational organisations choose to harmonise all their international practices with EU laws because it is practical to do so. On the importance of distinguishing between

As in the Digital Services Act, there is a proportional and cumulative logic in the Intelligence Act in imposing obligations as risks increase. In the Digital Services Act, systemic risk plays a central role, while in the Artificial Intelligence Act four levels of risk are identified: unacceptable risk, high risk, limited and minimal risk.[19] The two opposite poles are the systems that have an unacceptable risk and are therefore banned, and the systems that have only a minimal risk and are therefore only subject to transparency obligations to make users aware of their use. More problematic are the high–risk systems[20] that lie between the two identified poles and are those for which strict obligations are imposed before they are placed on the market[21] and subsequent monitoring.[22]

Comparison and coordination with the Artificial Intelligence Act will be inevitable when analysing to what extent and in what way the Digital Services Act can make a concrete contribution to anti–discrimination protection. Discrimination, in fact, now

---

artificial intelligence systems and outputs produced by the systems, in particular for the purpose of determining the scope of the Artificial Intelligence Act, see Orlando (2022), p. 346.

[19] This is stated in COM (2020) 65 final, p. 19. There, it moves in the direction of banning risks considered by the community to be socially unacceptable, while activities that do not generate any of the relevant risks should not fall within the scope of regulatory intervention. This approach has been criticised as it may reflect an unduly simplified view, according to which the purpose of regulation is solely to minimise the "most significant" risks. On this point see Yeung (2020), p. 1. The author states that a much finer scale for risk assessment would be required, rather than adopting a binary classification system to determine whether a particular artificial intelligence application falls within the regulatory framework.

[20] Artificial intelligence systems identified as high-risk include artificial intelligence technology used in: critical infrastructures (e.g. transport), that could put the life and health of citizens at risk; educational or vocational training, that may determine the access to education and professional course of someone's life (e.g. scoring of exams); safety components of products, (e.g. artificial intelligence application in robot-assisted surgery); employment, management of workers and access to self-employment (e.g. CV-sorting software for recruitment procedures); essential private and public services (e.g. credit scoring denying citizens opportunity to obtain a loan); law enforcement that may interfere with people's fundamental rights (e.g. evaluation of the reliability of evidence); migration, asylum and border control management (e.g. verification of authenticity of travel documents); administration of justice and democratic processes (e.g. applying the law to a concrete set of facts). On this point, refer to Annexes to the Artificial Intelligence Act. https://digital-strategy.ec.europa.eu/en/library/proposal-regulation-laying-down-harmonised-rules-artificial-intelligence.

[21] See, in particular, Article 43 of the Artificial Intelligence Act. The provision has been criticised by those who have pointed out its circularity, highlighting that conformity assessments based on internal control are sufficient for stand-alone artificial intelligence systems that comply with the Artificial Intelligence Act, but how can suppliers know whether a specific artificial intelligence system is compliant before the assessment is carried out? In these terms Mökander et al. (2021), p. 11.

[22] These are auditing processes through which an entity's present or past behaviour and performance are assessed for consistency with reference standards. See on this point LaBrie and Steinke (2019); Having laid the foundations for a uniform discipline, there is no getting away from outlining an articulated framework that considers the diverse nature of artificial intelligence systems. Many high-risk artificial intelligence systems are used as security components of existing products. In this case, also to avoid duplication, no specific conformity assessments are carried out, but the conformity assessments already provided for in each sector will be considered. See Brown et al. (2021), p. 9.

also depends on how one interacts with algorithms and artificial intelligence systems, which are increasingly used by digital service intermediaries.[23]

Through the comparison between the Digital Services Act and the Proposed Artificial Intelligence Act, the work aims to demonstrate under what conditions the risk–based approach can be an opportunity for the future.

1.2 Non-discrimination in Digital Service Intermediation

The European Union's attention to discrimination in the digital environment can already be seen in the European Parliament Resolution of 20 October 2020 on the Digital Services Act and fundamental rights issues posed (2020/2022(INI)). In this Resolution it is stated that the principle of non-discrimination needs to be ingrained at the core of a successful and durable European Union policy on digital services. In contributing to anti-discrimination protection, the Digital Services Act is in line with the European Declaration on Digital Rights and Principles for the Digital Decade,[24] which is based on the proposal adopted by the Commission on 26 January 2022,[25] in the context of the Digital Decade Policy Programme 2030.[26]

The general objectives of the Digital Decade Policy Programme 2030 include facilitating fair and non-discriminatory conditions for users during the digital transformation[27] and the European Declaration on Digital Rights and Principles for the Digital Decade calls for a model of digital transformation that strengthens the human dimension of the digital ecosystem. Suffice it to mention the provisions of Chap. 2

[23] Zuiderveen Borgesius (2020), p. 2.

[24] European Declaration on Digital Rights and Principles for the Digital Decade, Brussels, COM (2022) 28 final. https://ec.europa.eu. The Declaration shows that solidarity and inclusion in the digital world cannot go without excellent digital connectivity for everyone, wherever they live and whatever their income. The Declaration is clear in specifying that inclusion is achieved by guaranteeing the right to education, training and lifelong learning in order to acquire basic digital skills and otherwise necessary to actively participate in the economy, society and democratic processes. For effective inclusion are also essential equitable, fair, healthy and safe working conditions, protecting the worker in the digital environment as in the physical workplace and ensuring that everyone has the opportunity to disconnect and enjoy work-life balance guarantees. Everyone should have access to all key public services online across the Union. Nobody is to be asked to provide data more often than necessary when accessing and using digital public services. Compare Tommasi (2022), p. 168, Alfonsi (2022), p. 707, Della Rocca (2022), p. 250.

[25] Communication from the Commission to the European Parliament, the Council, the European Economic and Social Committee and the Committee of the Regions—Establishing a European Declaration on Digital rights and principles for the Digital Decade, COM (2022) 27 final. https://ec.europa.eu.

[26] Decision (EU) 2022/2481 of the European Parliament and of the Council of 14 December 2022 establishing the Digital Decade Policy Programme 2030 in https://commission.europa.eu. Important insights can also be drawn from the study of the Flemish Government, Department of Economy, Science and Innovation Reflections on 2030 Digital Compass: the European way for the Digital Decade, 2021. https://publicaties.vlaanderen.be/view-file/43500.

[27] See Article 3(i).

of the Declaration, where the title already refers to "Solidarity and inclusion", confirming that the online dimension of our lives cannot ignore being supportive and inclusive. Technological solutions must also, therefore, enable the exercise of rights, promote inclusion and pursue a digital transformation that leaves no one behind. The declaration aims to promote a digital transformation that includes elderly people, persons with disabilities, or marginalised, vulnerable or disenfranchised people and those who act on their behalf.[28]

The need for inclusive digital transformation is also underlined by the European Parliament Resolution of 13 December 2022 on the digital divide: the social differences created by digitalization,[29] where it is highlighted that the potential of new technologies is ambivalent, as depending on how they are used and regulated, they can either help create a more inclusive society and reduce inequities, or they can amplify existing inequalities and create new forms of discrimination.[30]

The Digital Services Act is complementary to the Regulation (EU) 2022/1925 of the European Parliament and of the Council of 14 September 2022 on contestable and fair markets in the digital, known as Digital Markets Act, which is primarily aimed at protecting smaller European competitors against US "big tech".[31]

In the Digital Markets Act, despite some explicit references also to the protection of end users, the latter are only indirectly benefited. The purpose of the Digital Markets Act is to provide for "ex ante" enforcement actions to ensure competitive markets under the threat of very large fines. In this way, smaller competitors would no longer need to resort to the current system of ex post enforcement against abuse of monopoly power, which is believed to be insufficiently equipped to deal with digital monopoly power.[32]

The Digital Services Act, on the other hand, concerns the relationship between digital service intermediaries and users.[33]

---

[28] COM (2022) 28 final, p. 3, where we read that digital transformation can cause new discrimination. To limit this possibility, it is necessary that all market actors benefiting from the digital transformation assume their social responsibilities and make a fair and proportionate contribution to the costs of public goods, services and infrastructures, for the benefit of all Europeans.

[29] https://www.europarl.europa.eu/doceo/document/TA-9-2022-0438_EN.pdf.

[30] European Parliament Resolution of 13 December 2022 on the digital divide, p. 3.

[31] Bergkamp (2021), p. 152.

[32] Bergkamp (2021), p. 152, Marsden and Brown (2023), p. 17, say that non-discrimination has become an essential item in the regulatory toolkit when analysing barriers in both access and app store markets. Under the Digital Markets Act, it has now been codified in a form that will permit further extensions of this principle, as for instance in interoperability between messaging apps and APIs.

[33] See whereas 3 of the Digital Services Act, where it reads that: ‹‹responsible and diligent behaviour by providers of intermediary services is essential for a safe, predictable and trustworthy online environment and for allowing Union citizens and other persons to exercise their fundamental rights guaranteed in the Charter of Fundamental Rights of the European Union in particular the freedom of expression and of information, the freedom to conduct a business, the right to non-discrimination and the attainment of a high level of consumer protection››.

The different, albeit complementary, aims of the two measures also justify the different way in which the problematic profiles relating to non-discrimination are addressed.

In the Digital Markets Act, non-discrimination is understood as the defence of "contestability", in the digital sector,[34] between the products and services offered by different "business users".[35]

Discrimination is taken into account in relation to the conditions of access and permanence of "business users" in the digital market.[36]

This discrimination may depend mainly on two factors, in respect of which the Digital Markets Act aims to intervene with prohibitions.[37]

Firstly, the gatekeepers have a significant impact on the internal market, acting as an important gateway for business users to reach end users and benefit from a durable and entrenched position in their operations.[38] At the same time, the gatekeepers have a dual role as a provider of core platform services whereby it provides a core platform service to its business users, while also competing with those same Business users in the provision of the same or similar services or products to the same end users.[39]

In view of this situation, Article 6(d) of the Digital Markets Act, precisely to avoid discrimination, provides that gatekeeper shall refrain from treating more favourably in ranking services and products offered by the gatekeeper itself or by any third party belonging to the same undertaking compared to similar services or products of third party and apply fair and non-discriminatory conditions to such ranking.

The second factor is well highlighted by whereas 56 of the Digital Markets Act, where it is noted that the providers of online search engine services collect these data from searches undertaken on their own online search engine service and, where applicable, searches undertaken on the platforms of their downstream commercial partners. Access by gatekeepers to such ranking, query, click and view data constitutes an important barrier to entry and expansion, which undermines the contestability of online search engine services.

To safeguard a fair commercial environment and protect the contestability of the digital sector, the gatekeepers, according to Article 6(j) of the Digital Markets Act, must provide access on fair, reasonable and non-discriminatory terms, to these ranking, query, click and view data in relation to free and paid search generated by consumers on online search engine services to other providers of such services, so

---

[34] See whereas 8 of the Digital Markets Act.

[35] For the definition of "business user" see Article 2 of the Digital Markets Act.

[36] Compare Hovenkamp (2023), Crémer et al. (2019), Graef (2019), p. 448, Attri and Bapuji (2021).

[37] Brouwer (2021), where it is hoped that the European Commission will engage in a "regulatory dialogue" with the gatekeeper to ensure an effective implementation of the prohibition of discriminatory rankings. The author has also dealt with these issues before. See Brouwer (2020).

[38] See whereas 24 of the Digital Markets Act.

[39] See whereas 43 and whereas 48 of the Digital Markets Act. For the definition of gatekeeper, please refer to Article 2 of the Digital Markets Act.

that these third-party providers can optimise their services and contest the relevant core platform services.[40]

The Digital Services Act looks at the risk of discrimination from the point of view of the user who may be adversely affected in accessing the digital market and digital services or in the governance of the services themselves and of the content disseminated. Specifically, it is these aspects, which are particularly delicate also due to the increasingly frequent use of artificial intelligence systems, that will be the subject of the analysis proposed in the following chapters.

The aim is to demonstrate that the Digital Services Act plays an important role in protecting against the risk of discrimination in the digital market because it equates discriminatory content with illicit content, regulates the so-called notice and takedown mechanism in detail, makes digital service intermediaries responsible and considers as a systemic risk any actual or foreseeable negative effects on the right not to be discriminated against by providers of very large online platforms and of very large online search engines.

The analysis of the Digital Services Act will be conducted with a non-sectoral approach, but a systemic one that is attentive to the contribution that, in terms of protection against discrimination, can also be made by more general and transversal regulations, such as those on data protection, unfair commercial practices and artificial intelligence.

The proposed comparison aims to establish a coherent regulatory framework against the main criticisms of the European Union's recent legislative activity, which is characterised by measures that are not always sufficiently harmonised.

The focus on the potential discriminatory scope of the intermediation of digital services is a strategic observation angle of the dangers that may affect the digital transformation as a whole.

The proposed perspective is of a technologically advanced future, risky but not dangerous, as one must be aware not only of human limitations but also of those of artificial intelligence systems, which cannot be entrusted with rights that are indispensable for sustainable development.

References

Achleitner RA (2022) Der Digital Services Act als risikobasierte Regulierung – Zu den Auswirkungen des risikobasierten Ansatzes des DSA auf Desinformation und den Grundrechtsschutz. MR–Int 4:114–121

Adamski D (2018) Lost on the digital platform: Europe's legal travails with the Digital Single Market. Common Market Law Review 55:719–752

Alfonsi R (2022) La EU Interinstitutional Declaration on digital rights and principles del 14.11.2022. Persona e Mercato. Osservatorio OGID 4:707–708

Arbia E (2020) Digital package: verso la regolamentazione delle piattaforme online. Giustizia insieme. https://www.giustiziainsieme.it/it/diritto-e-innovazione/1404-la-regolamentazione-delle-piattaforme-online?hitcount=0

[40] See whereas 56 of the Digital Markets Act.

Attri PS, Bapuji H (2021) Digital discrimination in sharing economy at the base of the pyramid. In Qureshi I, Bhatt B, Shukla DM (eds) Sharing economy at the base of the pyramid. Springer, Singapore, pp 221–249

Bergkamp P (2021) The proposed EU digital markets act: a new era for the digital economy in Europe. Eur Company Law 18:152–161

Brouwer D (2020) A non-discrimination principle for rankings in app stores. https://policyreview.info/articles/analysis/non-discrimination-principle-rankings-app-stores

Brouwer D (2021) Towards a ban of discriminatory rankings by digital gatekeepers? Reflections on the proposal for a Digital Markets Act. https://policyreview.info/articles/news/towards-ban-discriminatory-rankings-digital-gatekeepers-reflections-proposal-digital

Brown S, Davidovic J, Hasan A (2021) The algorithm audit: scoring the algorithms that score us. Big Data Soc. https://doi.org/10.1177/205395172098

Busch C, Mak V (2021) Putting the digital services act in context: bridging the gap between EU consumer law and platform regulation. J Eur Consumer Market Law 109:1–14

Caggiano G (2021) La proposta di Digital Service Act per la regolazione dei servizi e delle piattaforme online nel diritto dell'Unione europea. Annuali Aisdue 1:1–29

Camardi C (2021) Contratti digitali e mercati delle piattaforme. Un promemoria per il civilista. Jus Civile 4:870–919

Chamberlain J (2023) The risk-based approach of the European Union's proposed artificial intelligence regulation: some comments from a tort law perspective. Eur J Risk Regulation 14:1–13

Cornils M (2020) Designing platform governance: a normative perspective on needs, strategies, and tools to regulate intermediaries. https://algorithmwatch.org

Crémer J, de Montjoye YA, Schweitzer H (2019) Competition policy for the digital era. https://ec.europa.eu/competition/publications/reports/kd0419345enn.pdf

De Franceschi A, Schulze R, Graziadei M, Pollicino O, Riente F, Sica S, Sirena P (eds.) (2019), Digital Revolution – New Challenges for Law. Data Protection, Artificial Intelligence, Smart Products, Blockchain Technology and Virtual Currencies. CH Beck and Nomos, München - Baden-Baden

Della Rocca F (2022) Il contratto tra tecnologia e diritti fondamentali. Tecnologie e Diritto 2:250–276

Efroni Z (2020) Gaps and opportunities: the rudimentary protection for "data–paying consumers" under new EU consumer protection law. J Eur Consumer Market Law 57:799–830

Gatt L, Caggiano IA (2022) Consumers and digital environments as a structural vulnerability relationship. Eur J Privacy Law Technol 8:8–16

Graef I (2019) Differentiated treatment in platform–to–business relations: EU competition law and economic dependence. Yearbook of Eur Law 38:448–499. https://doi.org/10.1093/yel/yez008

Hovenkamp E (2023) Platform discrimination against rivals: an economic framework for antitrust enforcement. J Corp Law 12:1–24

Iacovelli D, Fontana M (2022) Nuove sfide della tecnologia e gestione dei rischi nella proposta di regolamento europeo sull'intelligenza artificiale: set di training, algoritmi e qualificazione dei dati. Profili critici. Diritto dell'economia 109:107–138

Iannarelli A (2022) La regolazione privatistica delle relazioni di mercato nell'attuale contesto. Rivista critica del diritto privato 3:297–321

Janssen A, Lehmann M, Schulze R (eds) (2023) The future of European Private Law. Nomos Verlagsgesellschaft, Baden-Baden

LaBrie RC, Steinke GH (2019) Towards a framework for ethical audits of AI algorithms. In: 25th Americas conference on information systems AMCIS. https://web.archive.org/web/20200318085901id_/, https://aisel.aisnet.org/cgi/viewcontent.cgi?article=1398&context=amcis2019. Accessed 19 July 2023

Lind RA (2002) Disintermediation. In: Jones S (ed) Encyclopedia of new media: An essential reference to communication and technology. SAGE Publications, Chicago. https://doi.org/10.4135/9781412950657

Lopez-Tarruella A (2001) A European community regulatory framework for electronic commerce. Common Market Law Rev 30:1337–1384
Mândrescu D (2020) EU competition law and the digital economy: protecting free and fair competition in an age of technological (r)evolution. Eleven International Publishing, Chicago
Mantelero A (2023) Fundamental rights impact assessment in the DSA. In: Van Hoboken J, Quintais JP, Appelman N, Fahy R, Buri I, Straub M (eds). Putting the digital services act into practice. Enforcement, access to justice, and global implications. Verfassungsblog gGmbH, Berlin
Marsden CT, Brown I (2023), App stores, antitrust and their links to net neutrality: a review of the European policy and academic debate leading to the EU Digital Markets Act. https://policyreview.info/articles/analysis/app-stores-antitrust-net-neutrality-eu-digital-markets-act. Accessed 19 July 2023
Mökander J, Axente M, Casolari F, Floridi L (2021) Conformity assessments and post-market monitoring: a guide to the role of auditing in the proposed European AI regulation. Mind Mach 32:241–268
Mollo A (2021) La vulnerabilità tecnologica. Neurorights ed esigenze di tutela: profili etici e giuridici. Eur J Privacy Law Technol 7:199–210
Moscon V (2020) Free circulation of information and online intermediaries—Replacing One "value gap." Int Rev Intellect Property Compet Law 51:977–982
Narciso M (2019) The regulation of online reviews in European consumer law. Eur Rev Private Law 27:557–581
Orlando S (2022) Regole di immissione sul mercato e «pratiche di intelligenza artificiale» vietate nella proposta di Artificial Intelligence Act. Persona e Mercato 3:346–367
Panetta R (2019) Il ruolo dell'internet service provider e i profili di responsabilità civile. Responsabilità civile e previdenza 84:1017–1035
Passaglia P (2021) La problematica definizione dell'accesso a Internet e le sue ricadute su esclusioni sociali e potenziali discriminazioni. Media Laws 5:1–19
Pérez–Escolar M, Canet F (2022) Research on vulnerable people and digital inclusion: toward a consolidated taxonomical framework, in Universal Access in the Information Society. https://doi.org/10.1007/s10209-022-00867-x
Petruso R (2002) Danno da prodotto difettoso e responsabilità delle piattaforme di e-commerce: uno sguardo oltreoceano. Persona e Mercato 4:59–78
Ponzanelli G (2002) Verso un diritto uniforme per la responsabilità degli internet service providers? In: Stanzione P, Sica S (eds) Commercio elettronico e categorie civilistiche, Milan, Giuffrè, pp 363–379
Rabai B (2022) The role of technology and innovation in digital and social inclusion. The case of disability in a public perspective. Media Laws 6:199–211
Rid T (2022) Misure attive. Storia segreta della disinformazione. Luiss University Press, Rome
Schulze R, Staudenmayer D (2020) EU digital law: article–by–article commentary. Bloomsbury Publishing, New York
Scola S (2022) Digital Services Act: occasioni mancate e prospettive future nella recente proposta di regolamento europeo per il mercato unico dei servizi digitali. Contratto e impresa/Europa 1:127–172
Thomas S (2021) Horizontal restraints on platforms: how digital ecosystems nudge into rethinking the construal of the cartel prohibition. World Compet 44:53–80
Tommasi S (2022) La proposta di Dichiarazione europea sui diritti e i principi digitali per il decennio digitale COM (2022) 28 final del 26 gennaio 2022. Persona e Mercato. Osservatorio OGID 1:168–171
Turner BS (2006) Vulnerability and human rights. University Park, Pennsylvania University Press
Van Den Bergh R, Weber F (2021) The German Facebook Saga: Abuse of dominance or abuse of competition law? World Compet 44:29–52
Wielsch D (2019) Private law regulation of digital intermediaries. Eur Rev Private Law 27:197–220
Yeung K (2020) Response to European commission white paper on artificial intelligence. https://doi.org/10.2139/ssrn.3626915. Accessed 30 July 2023
Zuiderveen Borgesius FJ (2020) Strengthening legal protection against discrimination by algorithms and artificial intelligence. Int J Human Rights 24:1–22

Chapter 2
Digital Services Act and Non-discriminatory Digital Transformation

Abstract This chapter highlights the contribution of digital and artificial intelligence systems to economic growth and the geopolitical role of the European Union. It is however crucial not to be blinded by the innovation frenzy and to set the goal of a non-discriminatory digital transformation. The Digital Services Act tries to contribute to this goal by regulating intermediation in the field of digital services. The innovations of the Digital Services Act, also regarding the protection from non-discrimination, can be understood in comparison with the E-Commerce Directive 2000/31/EC. While placing itself in continuity with it and with some choices made in a different context from the current one, which was that of the early years of this century. The innovations that are relevant relate specifically to the fact that the Digital Services Act considers discriminatory content to be illegal and provides protection against it, both by regulating in detail the notice and takedown mechanism and by providing for greater responsibilities for digital service providers. The importance of the Digital Services Act is also linked to the fact that it qualifies as a systemic risk any actual or foreseeable negative effects for the exercise of the right not to be discriminated against.

Keywords Online platforms · Illegal content · Discriminatory content · Notice and takedown mechanism · E-commerce directive · Responsibilities of providers of digital services

2.1 Digital Services Act and Non-discrimination: Premise

The contribution of digital and artificial intelligence systems to economic growth and the geopolitical role of the European Union is clearly visible. It is however crucial not to be blinded by the innovation frenzy and to set the goal of a non-discriminatory digital transformation. The Digital Services Act contributes to this goal by regulating the intermediation in the field of digital services.[1]

---

[1] See Report on the Digital Services Act and fundamental rights issues posed 1.10.2020—(2020/2022(INI), Committee on Civil Liberties, Justice and Home Affairs Rapporteur. www.europarl.europa.eu. The European Parliament "calls on digital service providers to take content offline in a

S. Tommasi, *The Risk of Discrimination in the Digital Market*,
SpringerBriefs in Law, https://doi.org/10.1007/978-3-031-43640-6_2

The innovations of the Digital Services Act, also regarding protection from non-discrimination, can be understood in comparison with E-Commerce Directive.

The innovations that are relevant for our purposes relate specifically to the fact that the Digital Services Act considers discriminatory content as illegal and provides protection against it, both by regulating in detail the notice and takedown mechanism and by providing for greater responsibilities for digital service intermediaries. The importance of the Digital Services Act is also linked to the fact that it qualifies as systemic risks any actual or foreseeable negative effects for the exercise of the right not to be discriminated against.

It is therefore necessary to go into the details of the Digital Services Act to highlight what is new in the compared to the E-Commerce Directive and how these new elements can contribute to a non-discriminatory digital transformation.

2.2 Continuity with the Past and Novelty of the Digital Services Act

The E-Commerce Directive marked a key moment in the history of the Internet and was adopted at a different historical moment than the present one.[2] It was not a question, as today, of regulating a widespread phenomenon, but of promoting its development.[3] In this context, the activity of the information society service provider was of a mere technical, automatic and passive nature, which is consistent with not knowing and not controlling the information transmitted or stored.[4] This justified the exemptions from liability established in the E-Commerce Directive.

---

diligent, proportionate and non-discriminatory manner, and with due regard in all circumstances to the fundamental rights of the users and to take into account the fundamental importance of the freedom of expression and information in an open and democratic society with a view to avoiding the removal of content, which is not illegal; requests that digital service providers, which on their own initiative want to restrict certain legal content of their users, explore the possibility of labelling that content, rather than it taking offline, thus giving users the chance to choose to access that content on their own responsibility". On the importance of not becoming unconditionally fascinated by the undoubted extraordinariness of technological development see Grisi (2020), p. 545, Clarizia (2020), p. 687.

[2] For a recent analysis of the problems concerning electronic commerce see Finocchiaro (2023), p. 17, Piraino (2020), p. 7.

[3] See Tereszkiewicz (2018), p. 903.

[4] See whereas 30 of the Digital Services Act.

Today, innovation is such that the problem is, rather, to limit the enormous power of digital service providers[5] and reduce the risks of negative effects on democratic values[6] and people's fundamental rights.[7]

Furthermore, digital service providers are increasingly using artificial intelligence systems, so the impact of artificial intelligence systems on e-commerce also needs to be investigated.[8]

The foregoing confirms that, although the issue of intermediary liability is not in itself new, it constantly recurs in different terms with the emergence of new forms of intermediation in the internet sector.

The Digital Services Act is explicit in clarifying that, not only it does not prejudice the E-Commerce Directive, but it is based primarily on the same and the no general monitoring or active fact-finding obligations,[9] in compliance with Union law as interpreted by the Court of Justice of the European Union.[10]

Nothing in the Digital Services Act should be construed as an imposition of a general monitoring obligation or active fact-finding obligation, or as a general obligation for providers to take proactive measures in relation to illegal content.[11]

This is not enough, however, to say that there are no new elements. A change, moreover, was desired by those who criticised the E-Commerce Directive for not

[5] Eifert et al. (2021), p. 987. See also Genç-Gelgeç (2022), p. 28. The author says that especially with the advent of Web 2.0, users have become more actively involved on the Internet, while intermediaries' societal, economic and political impact scales up accordingly.

[6] See Stark et al. (2020), p. 52.

[7] Communication in the digital world depends on internet intermediaries and, in particular, social networking platforms not only facilitate communication but also shape sociality. This is highlighted by Wielsch (2019), p. 197. On this point see De Franceschi (2018), p. 1, Caggiano (2021), p. 46.

[8] See Bawack et al. (2022), p. 297.

[9] See Article 8 of the Digital Services Act. Section 512 of the Digital Millennium Copyright Act (DMCA) was taken as a model. On this point see Petruso (2018), p. 511.

[10] Think, for example, Court of Justice of the European Union, 3 October 2019, in Case C18/18 Eva Glawischnig Piesczek v. Facebook Ireland Limite, on the relationship between the absence of a general control of the information that intermediary service providers transmit or store and the liability for information that has been previously declared unlawful. The Court considers that there is liability of the provider for information that has previously been declared unlawful only if it is information that does not require the hosting service provider an independent assessment of that content. About this judgment, Wielsch (2019), p. 197. The equivalent information must contain specific elements which are properly identified in the injunction, such as the name of the person concerned in the infringement previously determined, the circumstances in which that infringement was determined and equivalent content to that which was declared to be illegal. See on this point Genç-Gelgeç (2022), p. 25, where the author analytically examines the jurisprudence of the Court of Justice of the European Union on the liability of intermediaries.

[11] See whereas 30 of the Digital Services Act, where we read that providers of intermediary services should not be subject to a monitoring obligation with respect to obligations of a general nature.

keeping up with the pace of the Internet and for granting crucial discretion to intermediaries.[12] It is well known that E-Commerce Directive typifies the activities of providers and distinguishes between mere conduit, caching and hosting.[13]

One of the criticisms levelled at the E-Commerce Directive is that it set a standard of due diligence without paying attention to the structural differences and advantages between different digital service intermediaries. To overcome these limitations of the previous legislation, the Digital Services Act distinguishes digital services according to their size and their impact on the digital world.[14]

In particular, the Digital Services Act typifies additional intermediary figures compared to the E-Commerce Directive, in the knowledge that the considerable changes in the digital market over the last twenty years make the distinction between only three types of online activities no longer appropriate.[15]

In the Digital Services Act, in fact, in addition to the distinction between mere conduit, caching and hosting, we also find the distinction between very large online search engines and online or very large online platforms. The latter are those that provide their services to an average monthly number of recipients active in the European Union of 45 million or more.[16]

Furthermore, a proportional and cumulative logic is outlined in the imposition of obligations, which increase and add up as the providers of intermediation services are qualified as hosting, very large online search engines and online or very large online platforms.[17]

Let us now go into the detail and focus on the innovations noted for the purposes of protection against the risk of discrimination in the digital marketplace.

---

[12] Genç-Gelgeç (2022), p. 25.

[13] Tereszkiewicz (2018), p. 903. The author notes that two main approaches to platform liability are identified and discussed: on the one hand, the idea of general platform liability provisions, exemplified by the draft discussion on digital platforms; on the other hand, sector-specific provisions densely regulating business models based on digital platforms.

[14] Genç-Gelgeç (2022), p. 33.

[15] Compare Panetta (2019), p. 1019, Salanitro (2020), p. 1246.

[16] See Article 33(1) of the Digital Services Act.

[17] The sub-category of online platforms is made up of hosting service providers who not only store the information provided by the recipients of the service at their request, but also disseminate this information to the public. That is, they make it available to a potentially unlimited number of people or make it easily accessible to users, regardless of whether they access. The liability for mere conduit is regulated by Article 4 of the Digital Services Act, which reproduces the well-known contents of Article 12 of the E-Commerce Directive. Also, in the case of the provision of an information society service consisting in caching, Article 5 of the Digital Services Act reproduces the content of Article 13 of the E-Commerce Directive, stating the well-known hypotheses of exemption from liability that must occur at the same time. The provider is also exempt from liability for storing, on a long-term basis, information provided by a recipient of the service, so-called hosting activity pursuant to Article 5 of the Digital Services Act, provided that he is unaware of the unlawfulness of the activity or information, of the facts or circumstances that make such unlawfulness manifest and provided that, in the event that he becomes aware of such facts, he acts immediately to remove the information or to disable access to it. These are alternative conditions of exemption based on the provider's actual knowledge of the offence. In fact, it is enough for one of the two conditions to be met for the provider to benefit from exemption from liability.

2.3 Illegal Content and Discriminatory Content

The Digital Services Act considers discriminatory content as illegal in itself.[18] It is therefore necessary to focus on the notion of illegal content, which is laid down in Article 3(h) of the Digital Services Act and which has been subject to repeated variations during the regulation's approval process.[19]

In COM (2020) 825 final, i.e. in the December 2020 version of the Proposal for a Regulation on a Single Market for Digital Services,[20] it was stated that «illegal content means any information, which, in itself or by its reference to an activity, including the sale of products or provision of services is not in compliance with Union law or the law of a Member State, irrespective of the precise subject matter or nature of that law».

The first problem noted with reference to this wording was that, although there may be a certain level of harmonisation at European level in relation to certain types of particularly serious illegal online content, differences between the various national legislations cannot be excluded. The subject of illegal content, in fact, has so far been governed by sectoral directives that by their very nature are likely to be implemented, in some respects, differently in the various national contexts. The provider should, therefore, be familiar with the regulations in force in the various states and adopt different policies, which are obviously not compatible with the cross-border nature of his activity and the objective of avoiding disparities in treatment for the same content.

The highlighted problem, neglected in the amendments of 20 January 2022,[21] was instead taken into account in the version of Article 2 of the Digital Services Act proposed on 15 June 2022, where it is stated that «illegal content means any information, which, in itself or in relation to an activity, including the sale of products or the provision of services, is not in compliance with Union law or the law of any Member State which is in compliance with Union law, irrespective of the precise subject matter or nature of that law».[22] Emphasis is not placed on the provisions of the Member States in general, but on those that comply with European Union law.

---

[18] See whereas 30 of the Digital Services Act. For an overview of the fight against illegal content on online platforms in the EU, see Ullrich (2021), p. 225.The author considers that the fight against unlawful content on online platforms in the EU is hampered by fragmented and outdated laws and reviews seven problematic areas—defamation, hate speech, terrorist content, copyright, counterfeit, unsafe products and food.

[19] See Achleitner (2023), p. 114. On the approval process of the Digital Services Act see also Tommasi (2022a, b), p. 698.

[20] In https://eur-lex.europa.eu.

[21] The European Parliament's Amendments to the Proposal for a Regulation on a Single Market for Digital Services, adopted on 20 January 2022. https://www.europarl.europa.eu/doceo/document/TA-9-2022-0014_IT.html.

[22] For the text of the Article 2 of the Digital Services Act proposed on 15 June 2022, see: www.europarl.europa.eu/meetdocs/2014_2019/plmrep/COMMITTEES/IMCO/DV/2022/06-15/DSA_2020_0361COD_EN.pdf.

In the July 2022 version of the Digital Services Act, a step backwards was taken with respect to the objective of fully harmonising the rules applicable to intermediary services in the internal market,[23] given the reference to the configurability of illegal content insofar as it does not comply with the regulatory provisions of any Member State, without the explicit reference to the conformity of such regulations with European Union law. Thus, the questions that the provision proposed in June 2022 seemed to have overcome were raised again.

The final choice of the Digital Services Act, however, in its version of 19 October 2022, is to give prominence, in the definition of illegal content, to the infringement of the law of any Member State only if it complies with European Union law. And besides, the reasons for the non-acceptance of the June 2022 amendment are understandable if one considers that the necessary prominence, for the purposes of the regulation, of illegality arising from the violation of provisions of Member States that comply with European Union law can be deduced from other data.

The reference to national law complying with European Union law can be found, for instance, in whereas 12 of the Digital Services Act. The latter is explicative of what is to be understood by illegal content, specifying that this concept should in particular be understood as referring to information, irrespective of its form, that under the applicable law is either itself illegal, such as illegal hate speech or terrorist content and unlawful discriminatory content, or that the applicable rules render illegal in view of the fact that it relates to illegal activities.[24]

There are, therefore, two types of illegal content: those that are defined as illegal in themselves, and those that are illegal as they relate to illegal activities. In particular, whereas 12 of the Digital Services Act specifies that the concept of 'illegal content' should be defined broadly to cover information relating to illegal content, products, services, and activities.

Therefore, unless one wishes to assume that legal hate speech or legal terrorist and discriminatory content can be configured, the rule must be interpreted to mean

---

[23] Whereas 9 of the Digital Services Act specifies that the aim is to harmonise the rules applicable to intermediary services in the internal market. Accordingly, Member States should not adopt or maintain additional national requirements relating to the matters falling within the scope of the Digital Services Act, unless explicitly provided for in the Digital Services Act, since this would affect the direct and uniform application of the fully harmonised rules applicable to providers of intermediary services in accordance with the objectives of the Digital Services Act. See also Article 1 of the Digital Services Act where it points out that the aim of this Regulation is to contribute to the proper functioning of the internal market for intermediary services by setting out harmonised rules for a safe, predictable and trusted online environment that facilitates innovation and in which fundamental rights enshrined in the Charter, including the principle of consumer protection, are effectively protected.

[24] Together with the European Democracy Action Plan, the Media Action Plan and, most recently, the Media Freedom Act, the Digital Services Act aims to represent a turning point in the fight against digital hate speech, focusing on the provision of appropriate procedural guarantees in favour of users. See Tommasi (2021), p. 213. Among the first states to react to hate speech are Germany, which adopted the so-called Facebook Act, i.e. The Network Enforcement Act. https://www.gesetze-im-internet.de. France approved, in December 2018, the Law n° 2018–1202 of 22 December 2018 on combating the manipulation of l'information. https://www.legifrance.gouv.fr. Also of relevance is the debate on the UK's Online Safety Bill, on which we refer to Trengove et al. (2022).

that not only content defined by law as legal is relevant for the purposes of the Regulation, but also content that, although not explicitly defined as illegal, refers to illegal activities.[25]

But there is more. It is also necessary to have regard to what is laid down in Article 34 of the Digital Services Act, which explicitly distinguishes between illegal content and negative effects on the exercise of fundamental rights and the right to non-discrimination, giving these negative effects self-importance. Thus, even abuses that do not take the form of unlawful content, when they affect the rights taken into consideration by Article 34, i.e. also the right not to be discriminated against, fall within the scope of the Digital Services Act. While this may provide greater protection, it also makes the boundaries of what constitutes abuse that is not illegal too labile, with inevitable difficulties in balancing it with other rights, such as the right to freedom of expression.

Whereas 12 of the Digital Services Act also specifies that the concept of illegal content should broadly reflect the existing rules in the offline environment. The general view is that what is illegal offline should also be illegal online.

On this point, it must be emphasised that, although this is an acceptable perspective, it cannot be conclusive.

In fact, situations may occur online that ontologically cannot be implemented offline or that have a scope of harm that cannot be compared to that which can be had in a non-digital dimension.

It is therefore necessary to recognise the specificities of online illicit offences while avoiding considering them part of a microsystem that responds to its own rules that are completely detached from the general ones and, above all, from the values and principles that inspire those rules.

The Digital Services Act, as announced, provides protection against illegal content both by regulating in detail the so-called notice and takedown mechanism and by providing for greater responsibilities for digital service intermediaries. Regarding these aspects, it is necessary, at this point, to go into detail.

2.4 Right to Non-discrimination and Notice and Takedown Mechanism

The right to non-discrimination may be violated by an unjustifiable removal of the content that one would like to disseminate, but also, on the contrary, by the failure to provide for mechanisms to combat illegal content.[26] At stake is the dignity of

[25] Whereas 12 of the Digital Services Act lists some illegal activities and these include, but are not limited to, the sharing of images depicting child sexual abuse, the unlawful non-consensual sharing of private images, online stalking, the sale of non-compliant or counterfeit products, the sale of products or the provision of services in infringement of consumer protection law, the non-authorised use of copyright protected material, the illegal offer of accommodation services or the illegal sale of live animals.

[26] See whereas 41 of the Digital Services Act.

the human person potentially exposed to the ferocity of the digital world and the indelible nature of the traces we leave online of our life fragments.[27]

The fact that the Digital Services Act equates discriminatory content with illegal content means that the risk of discrimination can also be protected by the mechanism of the notice and takedown and the innovations on this point in the Digital Services Act.

Significant novelties, compared to the E-Commerce Directive, are to be found in the governance of online content through the so-called notice and takedown mechanism, both in the case where the notification of illegal content is made by the competent Authorities, and in the case where it comes from private individuals.

About the case that it is the competent national judicial and administrative Authorities that issue an order to the provider to counteract illegal content, Article 9 of the Digital Services Act prescribes that such orders must have specific requirements. It is therefore not enough to simply issue a general warning, but the provider must only act, in order to prevent incurring liability, after receiving an order containing the conditions set out in Article 9 of the Digital Services Act.[28]

In the Digital Services Act, in line with E-Commerce Directive, the removal of content or the disabling of access can take place without prior notification by the competent Authorities and upon notification by any person or entity. Also in this case, however, notifications must comply with the mechanism specifically regulated by Article 16 of the Digital Services Act, which aims to overcome the many interpretative doubts posed by Article 14 of E-Commerce Directive and addressed in numerous cases by the Court of Justice of the European Union.[29]

Article 14 of the E-Commerce Directive, by not clarifying when the provider's knowledge of the unlawfulness was effective and when the unlawfulness of the activity or information was manifest, had in fact given rise to numerous disputes. On this point, Article 16 of the Digital Services Act is more detailed and states that notices containing all the elements required by Article 16(2) shall be considered to give rise to actual knowledge or awareness for the purposes of Article 6 of the Digital Services Act.

In such cases, there is an obligation to remove illegal content or to disable access to it, if a diligent hosting service provider can identify illegal content without a thorough legal examination.[30]

---

[27] For a comparison of the treatment of hate speech in the United States and Europe see Kohl (2022), p. 1. See also Hong (2022), p. 76.

[28] Instead, based on Article 15 of the E-Commerce Directive, the provider's knowledge of suspected illegal activities or information entails the provider's obligation to inform the competent authorities without delay, and a generic request for information by the authorities is sufficient to oblige intermediary service providers to disclose to them the identification data of the recipients of the services.

[29] See, for example, Court of Justice of the European Union, 3 October 2019, Eva Glawischnig-Piesczek v. Facebook Ireland Limited. https://curia.europa.eu; Court of Justice of the European Union, 12 July 2011, L'Oréal v. eBay. https://curia.europa.eu.

[30] The specification was introduced by the June 2022 Amendments of the Digital Services Act.

Not any notification, therefore, but only the sufficiently precise and adequately substantiated one may be suitable to activate the content removal procedure. The information contained in the notice, moreover, must be such as to allow a diligent provider of hosting services to identify the illegality of the relevant activity or information without a detailed legal examination.[31]

In essence, even though they replicate the content of Articles 12, 13 and 14 of the E-Commerce Directive, Articles 4, 5 and 6 of the Digital Services Act add significant innovations to the liability of intermediary service providers, in that the complex and articulated system of obligations set out in the Digital Services Act must be considered as a whole.[32]

Since it has been established that hosting must remove illegal content or disable access to it, a specific set of obligations arise, which are regulated in detail by the Digital Services Act. According to Article 16, in fact, it is not enough for the hosting service to follow up on notifications that have the characteristics highlighted above. It is also necessary, once this is established that these notifications meet the requirements to open a detailed procedure, that also concerns the complaints handling process, which is a key element of procedural fairness in relations between platforms and their users.[33] It should not be overlooked that the articles concerning notice and action mechanisms, statement of reasons and notification of suspicions of criminal offences are applicable to providers of hosting services including online platforms, as provided for by the final text of the Digital Services Act of October 2022. Instead, these provisions were only applicable to the online platforms, and not also hosting services, as provided for by the Proposed Digital Services Act of December 2020.

The established procedure aims to avoid, precisely for the purposes of protection from possible discrimination, that access to digital services or the removal of intermediated content is simply based on the point of view of the platform, the speaker

---

[31] See Allen and Stockhem (2022). The authors think that the EU co-legislators made positive headway in improving this provision from the initial draft by introducing several safeguards. The notice and action mechanism in the final DSA still allows any individual or entity to submit a notice to alert the platform of the presence of allegedly illegal content. These notices, however, must be sufficiently precise and substantiated to the point that a provider can determine illegality without conducting a detailed legal examination.

[32] Tommasi (2022a, b), p. 925.

[33] See Busch (2020), p. 133, although with reference to the Regulation (EU) 2019/1150. Specific obligations are also prescribed in n the Statement of Reasons in Article 17 of the Digital Services Act. Providers of hosting services shall provide a clear and specific statement of reasons to any affected recipients of the service for any of the following restrictions imposed on the ground that the information provided by the recipient of the service is illegal content or incompatible with their terms and conditions: any restrictions of the visibility of specific items of information provided by the recipient of the service, including removal of content, disabling access to content, or demoting content; suspension, termination or other restriction of monetary payments; suspension or termination of the provision of the service in whole or in part; suspension or termination of the recipient of the service's account. The trustworthiness of flaggers is calibrated based on their origin, but also based on any previous flagging that turned out to be manifestly unfounded. In this logic, it is justified that online platforms must ensure that notifications submitted by so-called trusted flaggers, i.e., trustworthy flaggers under Article 22 of the Digital Services Act, are given priority.

himself or another person. A concern that recently animates a fervent debate that goes beyond European borders, as witnessed by the recent Texas House Bill 20, at the centre of the NetChoice, LLC v. Paxton case. In particular, there has been a split between the Fifth Circuit, which considered the constitutional law in the part where it prohibits platforms from removing content at their discretion, and a decision of the Eleventh Circuit that annulled a similar bill in the state of Florida.[34]

The balance between the protection of freedom of expression online and the fight against illegal content is, in the Digital Services Act, mainly entrusted to compliance with detailed procedural rules.[35] This is confirmed by the novelties introduced in terms of governance.[36]

In fact, a harmonised framework of authorities appointed to apply the Regulation is outlined, in the awareness that national strategies alone run the risk of resulting in a legal fragmentation that can only be an obstacle.[37]

The basic problem is that detailed procedural rules and novelties in terms of governance cannot solve the delicate problems that arise from the ontological immediacy and speed of the digital world in the face of the prudence and depth that decisions affecting individuals inevitably require.

For this it is necessary to deepen the profiles related to the increasingly active role of providers.

---

[34] NetChoice v. Paxton, No. 21-51178 (5th Cir. 2022). https://law.justia.com/cases/federal/appellate-courts/ca5/21-51178/21-51178-2022-09-16.html.

[35] Ortolani (2022), says that when observed in detail, the "procedure before substance" approach of the Digital Services Act leaves many questions unanswered. The final text of the Regulation contains compromises (e.g., concerning out-of-court dispute settlement), and blind spots (e.g., the absence of jurisdictional grounds for moderation-related litigation). However, the Digital Services Act also brings about important procedural improvements, concerning e.g., notice and action mechanisms and statements of reasons.

[36] The governance framework that the Digital Services Act outlines is an expression of the proportional and cumulative logic that pervades the entire legislation and that is further confirmed by the system of the sanctions that can be imposed, which is calibrated on the nature, seriousness, repetition and duration of the violation, according to a constant EU policy and entrusted mainly to a sanction as a percentage of the turnover; a sanction that in the Digital Services Act is always very low, even if higher than that provided for in previous measures. This is pointed out by Lasorella (2021), p. 8.

[37] The Digital Services Act discontinues the country-of-origin approach, providing for the same obligations for all platforms, regardless of their location, consistent with the fact that digital services are provided on a global scale and not to easily monitored and identified or identifiable markets. Equally, hindering would be an approach based on the country-of-origin principle, i.e., obligations that are affected by the place of establishment of those who disseminate content.

2.5 Digital Services Act and the Increasingly Active Role of Providers

Greater protection of the right not to be discriminated against can also be guaranteed by overcoming the barrier of the passive role of providers. This is the direction in which the Digital Services Act is moving, which, although formally remaining faithful to the structure of E-Commerce Directive, seems to delineate a figure of a provider that in most cases is necessarily active insofar as it carries out a series of activities that go beyond mere intermediation.[38]

Various provisions of the Digital Services Act highlight the fact that the activity of digital service providers is now increasingly carried out in such a way that it is difficult to consider them mere storers or carriers of the contents of others and, as such, not liable.

For example, Article 14 of the Digital Services Act states that providers of intermediary services shall include information on any restrictions that they impose in relation to the use of their service in respect of information provided by the recipients of the service, in their terms and conditions.

That information shall include information on any policies, procedures, measures and tools used for the purpose of content moderation, including algorithmic decision-making and human review, as well as the rules of procedure of their internal complaint handling system.

Providers of intermediary services shall act in a diligent, objective and proportionate manner in applying and enforcing those restrictions with due regard to the rights and legitimate interests of all parties involved, including the fundamental rights of the recipients of the service. The right not to be discriminated against certainly cannot be excluded from these rights.

In content moderation, discrimination can take place in different forms.

Firstly, discrimination may arise in the terms of use themselves, for example, when a specialised social media site restricts service to members of a certain religion. This form of discrimination is rare.

The second form of discrimination can result from deliberate enforcement, or non–enforcement, of the terms of use in a discriminatory way by platform's operators. Intentional direct discrimination in the enforcement of the terms of use results from a conscious decision to enforce a certain kind of violation or sanction a certain person or group of persons. Another deliberate form of discriminatory enforcement might be the delisting of an entity from search results because the entity represents an economic threat to the search engine operator. Unintentional indirect discrimination can arise from algorithmic and human bias resulting incertain kinds of content, or certain groups, being subject to stricter enforcement measures than other similar content or groups.[39]

---

[38] See D'Alfonso (2020), p. 108.

[39] See Maxwell (2022), p. 5.

Article 14 of the Digital Services Act, which among other things applies indiscriminately to all providers of intermediation services, seems to be interpreted in the sense that the provision of content moderation tools necessarily implies the performance of an activity, which among other things is particularly delicate as it may affect the rights and legitimate interests of all parties involved.[40]

In performing such a sensitive activity as the one just described, the intermediary of digital services cannot be exempt from liability. This is also to the benefit of service users in cases of discriminatory moderation of content or discriminatory application of the general conditions of the service offered.

Two references may be of interest at this point to identify the characteristics of an activity that is carried out in a diligent, objective and proportionate manner.

On the one hand, whereas 26 of the Digital Service Act and on the other hand, Article 3(3) of the so-called Open Internet Regulation.[41]

It is clear from whereas 26 that acting diligently must include acting in an non–discriminatory manner.

Article 3(3) of the Open Internet Regulation requires that providers of internet access services treat all traffic equally, when providing internet access services, without discrimination. The article requires that providers of internet access services shall treat all traffic equally, when providing internet access services, without discrimination and also requires that the traffic management measures shall be transparent, non-discriminatory, proportionate, and shall not be based on commercial considerations but on objectively different technical quality of service requirements of specific categories of traffic.[42]

The parallelism identified should not come as a surprise if one thinks of content moderation as a mechanism to make a form of Internet access possible.

Further specific obligations for providers of online platforms, incompatible with their merely "passive" role, are functional to achieving the public interest objectives pursued by the regulation.

---

[40] Further obligations are laid down in Article 12 of the Digital Services Act, which stipulates that providers of intermediary services shall designate a single point of contact to enable recipients of the service to communicate directly and rapidly with them, by electronic means and in a user-friendly manner, including by allowing recipients of the service to choose the means of communication, which shall not solely rely on automated tools. In addition to the obligations provided under E-Commerce Directive, providers of intermediary services shall make public the information necessary for the recipients of the service to easily identify and communicate with their single points of contact. This information shall be easily accessible and shall be kept up to date.

[41] Regulation (EU) 2015/2120 of 25 November 2015 laying down measures concerning open internet access and amending Directive 2002/22/EC on universal service and users' rights relating to electronic communications networks and services and Regulation (EU) 531/2012 on roaming on public mobile communications networks within the Union. https://eur-lex.europa.eu.

[42] See Maxwell (2022) p. 90. The author, commenting on Digital Services Act, notes that Online Regulation (EU) 2021/784 of 29 April 2021 on addressing the dissemination of terrorist content, imposes similar conditions on content moderation systems used to detect terrorist content, requiring that platforms publish their terms and conditions prohibiting the dissemination of terrorist content.

Among these objectives is the protection of minors also from possible discriminatory actions.[43] The protection of minors is an important policy objective of the European Union.[44]

The new Article 28 of the Digital Services Act is, in fact, specifically dedicated to the online protection of minors. Although, according to this article, providers of online platforms are not obliged ‹‹to process additional personal data to assess whether the recipient of the service is a minor››, they must implement adequate and proportionate measures to ensure ‹‹a high level of privacy, safety, and security of minors, on their service››.[45]

Providers of intermediary services that are primarily directed at minors, for example through the design or marketing of the service, or which are used predominantly by minors, should make particular efforts to render the explanation of their terms and conditions easily understandable to minors.[46]

Online platforms and very large online platforms cannot but play an active role if one considers all the new provisions in Section 4 of the Digital Services Act additional provisions applicable to providers of online platforms allowing consumers to conclude distance contracts with traders.

Article 30 of the Digital Services Act states that providers of online platforms, where they allow consumers to conclude distance contracts with traders, shall acquire the information necessary to identify the trader according to the so called "know your customer" model.[47]

Regarding this information, the role of online platforms cannot be merely "passive", as they shall make best efforts, pursuant to Article 30, to verify whether the information is reliable. This is the so–called traceability of traders, aimed at

---

[43] The problem is very complex and concerns, more generally, the relationship between minors and the use of digital technologies which include systems driven by artificial intelligence. On these issues, please refer to Bogani and Schafer (2022), p. 215. Here, in particular, there is a focus on the opportunity to dislodge the largely entrenched view of the child as an inferior rights holder. See Charisi et al. (2022), p. 1. The report focuses on linking scientific evidence with policymaking, to gain insights of the interplay between different stakeholders, and to go beyond the identification of ethical guidelines towards methods for practical future implementations.

[44] See COM/2020/624 final, Communication from the Commission to the European Parliament, the Council, the European Economic and Social Committee and the Committee of the Regions, Digital Education Action Plan 2021–2027. Resetting education and training for the digital age, in https://eur-lex.europa.eu. See also COM (2021) 142 final, Communication from the Commission to the European Parliament, the Council, the European Economic and Social Committee and the Committee of the Regions, EU strategy on the rights of the child. https://eur-lex.europa.eu. The Communication states that Children's rights are human rights. Every child in Europe and across the world should enjoy the same rights and be able to live free of discrimination, recrimination, or intimidation of any kind. This is a social, moral, and human imperative on which children—who account for almost one in five people living in the European Union and one in three in the world—and the wider community depends on.

[45] See Guibault et al. (2012).

[46] This is laid down in whereas 46 of the Digital Services Act. On this point, recital 83 with reference to the obligations towards minors of very large online platforms and of very large online search engines is also of particular interest.

[47] See Lodder and Carvalho (2022) p. 537.

combating the sale of counterfeit products online. The focus on trader traceability is also ensured by specific requirements on compliance by design, as online platform providers must design and organise their interface in such a way as to enable traders to provide consumers with certain relevant information to be identifiable.

But not only that, according to Article 31, providers of online platforms allowing consumers to conclude distance contracts with traders shall also make reasonable efforts to randomly check in any official, freely accessible, and machine-readable online database or online interface whether the products or services offered have been identified as illegal.[48]

The active role of the platform that enables distance contracts to be concluded with consumers is confirmed by further obligations incumbent on it, which also shall inform consumers who purchased the illegal product or service through its services of the fact that the product or service is illegal, the identity of the trader and any relevant means of redress.

It is as if the platform had to do everything possible to prevent the consumer from being damaged by the distance sale of illegal products or services, so that, if it does not have the contact details of all consumers concerned, it shall make publicly available and easily accessible on its online interface the information concerning the illegal product or service, the identity of the trader and any relevant means of redress.[49]

Further proof of the necessary active role of very large online platforms and online search engines can be found in Article 34 of the Digital Services Act. This provision stipulates the obligation to identify, analyse and assess any systemic risks stemming from the design, including algorithmic systems, functioning and use made of their services in the European Union.

This assessment must be specific and include risks related to the dissemination of illegal content through their services, possible negative effects on the exercise of fundamental rights, and intentional manipulation of the service; risks that must be assessed to manage and mitigate them.[50]

---

[48] This goes a step further than other, albeit more recent, European legislation. One example is Directive (EU) 2019/2161, which, following the introduction of Article 6a(b) of Directive 2011/83, requires the provider of an online marketplace to inform consumers whether the third party offering goods, services or digital content is a professional or not, and to warn them that if they do not deal with a professional, they will not benefit from the protection reserved for the consumer-professional relationship. And while it is true that the operator of the online marketplace does not guarantee the qualification of the third party, confining itself to reporting the declaration received from the latter, it is also true that the information on the subjective quality of the third party takes on such an important character that its omission may involve the extremes of a misleading commercial practice. See Tommasi (2020), p. 329. Hiwatashi Dos Santos (2020), p. 7. See Autorité de la concurrence, Decision 19-MC-01 of 3 January 2019 on a request for interim measures by Amadeus. http://www.autoritedelaconcurrence.fr. For the case of an invitation to purchase a product offered on an online marketplace, see point (f) inserted in Article 7(4) of Directive 2005/29. See also Versaci (2021), p. 590.

[49] See Article 24 sexies of the Digital Services Act.

[50] See Achleitner (2021), p. 1.

The recalled articles point out that the Digital Services Act, notwithstanding its aim to be in continuity with E-Commerce Directive, requires digital service intermediaries to carry out activities that are incompatible with their role as mere transmitters of the content of others. In fact, digital service providers have a series of obligations to which they cannot but be subject to responsibilities to protect the users of their services.

2.6 Towards Greater Responsibility of the Digital Service Providers

Greater protection of the right not to be discriminated against can be ensured by overcoming the idea of the predominantly passive role of providers. This in fact means that the provider cannot benefit from the liability exemptions provided by the E–Commerce Directive first and then by the Digital Services Act.[51]

The consequence of this is greater attention by the providers to the rights of people who might be harmed by their services and enforce their liability.[52]

It is important, therefore, to distinguish between a provider who has an active role and a provider who simply passes on information to others and, as such, has a so-called "passive" role. This distinction is not easy.[53]

One example is the case of comments to an online newspaper. The difficulties faced by the Court of Justice of the European Union in guaranteeing freedom of expression and, at the same time, the non–dissemination of illegal content are well known.[54]

---

[51] Compare Tommasi (2022a, b), p. 925.

[52] See Price (2021), p. 238. The author argues that platforms, in the social interactions they facilitate, establish online spaces that are governed by platform architecture and algorithms. These spaces present online hazards in the ways they curate content and interactions online, establishing environments that enable online harms.

[53] Such platforms are often much more than mere facilitators between the supplier and the user of goods, digital content or services, as many of them determine the terms and conditions, the price, manage the payment service, often taking a percentage as a processing fee. On this point see De Franceschi (2018), p. 1. Clarke (2022), says that the Digital Services Act imposes new obligations on online platforms and further defines their responsibility, particularly regarding marketplaces.

[54] For a detailed analysis of the European Court of Human Rights rulings on provider liability see Korpisaari (2022), p. 1. As is well known, greater rigour in recognising a purely technical role for the provider was found in The European Court of Human Rights (First Section), in the case of Delfi AS v. Estonia, Application no. 64569/09. On this judgment see Petruso (2018) p. 511. See also Court of Justice of the European Union, 11 September 2014, Sotiris Papasavvas v. O Fileleftheros Ltd, where it was ruled that the limits to civil liability provided for in Articles 12–14 of E-Commerce Directive do not apply to the case of a publisher that has a website on which the online version of a newspaper is published, if it has knowledge of and control over the published information, regardless of whether access to that website is free or for a fee. See also Court of Justice of the European Union in the Google AdWords case, Judgment of the Court (Grand Chamber) of 23 March 2010. On this judgment see Lahe and Turk (2012) p. 18.

On this point, the Digital Services Act clarified in whereas 13 that the comments section in an online newspaper could constitute such a feature, where it is ancillary to the main service represented by the publication of news under the editorial responsibility of the publisher, and therefore not necessarily qualifying the hosting as an online platform. In such cases, public dissemination may be a minor function in relation to another service and, for objective technical reasons, not usable without that other principal service.

This does not exclude, however, consistent with the Digital Services Act, the possibility of a liability of the provider[55] when, for example it makes a predefined evaluation grid of the services offered available to them or proceeds to categorize or elaborate a summary of the opinions or evaluations of users.[56]

However, the problems relating to the configurability of an active hosting also concern the activity that consists in optimizing the presentation of offers for sale or promoting them in the online market.[57] In whereas 23 and Article 6(3) of the Digital Services Act it is contemplated that if online platforms allow consumers to conclude distance contracts with commercial operators, they cannot benefit from the exemption from liability to the extent that they present the related information in such a way as to lead an average reasonably informed consumer to believe that they are aware of the information or control it, even though this may not be the case.[58]

This is a more stringent liability of the provider, a direction in which the Court of Justice of the European Union, (Grand Chamber) of 22 December 2022, Christian Louboutin v Amazon Europe Core Sàrl and Others is also moving.[59]

The Court of Justice of the European Union, in the preliminary ruling in question, clarifies the doubts of the national Courts by stating that the use of a trade mark

[55] Korpisaari (2022), p. 26, asserts that the liability exemption of the E-Commerce Directive is not applicable to holders of web discussion forums. However, this as such does not of itself constitute liability, because a basis for liability must always be found in the national legal order. The author specifies that the Digital Services Act does not directly apply to liability of website administrators, but rather applies to the intermediary services required to maintain a discussion site. A person who has been the target of hate speech can, under the Digital Services Act, ask the hosting service provider to remove illegal content when the website administrator does not respond or agree. The Digital Services Act offers the victim of illegal hate speech a faster and cheaper way to remove illegal offensive content than by filing a lawsuit. At the same time, however, the effects of the Digital Services Act on freedom of expression should be monitored.

[56] See Resta (2019), p. 199.

[57] See Court of Justice of the European Union, 12 July 2011, L'Oréal v. eBay- In the above case, the Court affirmed that eBay had not set up a mere online showcase, but, indeed, carried out an activity of organizing offers, promoting products, and indexing the search results such as to give it a different role from that which justifies the favor of the E-Commerce Directive. On this point see Eecke (2011), p. 1455. Also notable are Court of Justice of the European Union, 23 March 2010, Google v. Luis Vuitton; Court of Justice of the European Union, 7 August 2018, Cooperatieve Vereniging Snb-React U.A. v. Deepak Mehta. www.curia.europa.eu.

[58] In many cases, the consumer's attention is focused on the relationship. established with the platform acting as an intermediary, rather than on the second relationship concluded with the supplier of the good. In these terms, Versaci (2021), p. 586. Compare Palmieri (2019), p. 18, Martinelli (2023), p. 140.

[59] https://eur-lex.europa.eu.

by the operator of an online sales website incorporating, as well as that operator's own sales offerings, an online marketplace, may be prohibited by the proprietor of the trade mark if the activities of that operator of the platform lead the platform's consumer, who is normally well–informed and attentive, to establish a link between the operator's services and the trade mark in question.[60] According to the Court of Justice of the European Union, this is particularly the case when the customer has the impression that it is the platform operator itself that markets the goods bearing the mark on its own behalf.

The Court states that an informed and reasonably attentive user of a site may be deemed to establish a link between the services of the operator of that site and a trademark, where in the light of all the circumstances of the situation in question, that user may have the impression that the operator is itself markets, in its own name and on its own behalf, goods bearing that sign. In that regard, the following is relevant: the fact that trader uses a uniform method of presentation of the offers published on its website, displaying both the advertisements relating to the goods which it sells in its own name and on its own behalf and those relating to the goods offered by third-party sellers on that market; the fact that it places its logo as a renowned distributor on all those advertisements; and the fact that it offers third-party sellers, in the context of the marketing of the goods bearing that sign, additional services consisting, in particular, in the storage and dispatch of those goods.[61]

Of particular interest here is also Article 7 of the Digital Services Act because it confirms that the question of illegal content is closely linked to protection against discrimination. In fact, the rule provides that digital service intermediaries shall not be deemed ineligible for the exemptions from liability solely because they, in good faith and in a diligent manner, carry out voluntary own-initiative investigations into,

[60] In a similar vein had moved California Court of Appeal, 13 August 2020, 4th Dist., No. D075738 – Bolger v. Amazon.com Inc., available at https://www.courts.ca.gov. The Court, overturning the decision of first instance, held Amazon liable for the damage caused by a defective product sold through their site. The Court, while reaffirming the traditional approach according to which the operator of marketplace services is not liable for damages caused by products sold by others through the platform, did, however, specify that in the case at hand, Amazon, "an integral part of the overall producing and marketing enterprise", is "the only member of that enterprise reasonably available to the injured plaintiff" and, moreover, is in "the best position to ensure product safety". For a first comment on the judgment see Bertelli and Corsi (2020), Petruso (2022), p. 61. The author states that the California Court of Appeal in Bolger v. Amazon and the more recent decision rendered on 26 April 2021 in Loomis v. Amazon, 6th Dist., 466 shorten the hiatus between technical and social progress and legal reality in the new distribution chain of distance sales dominated by e-commerce platforms.

[61] In Italy, for example, the Court of Milan moved in a similar direction with its order of 19 October 2020, upholding the appeal brought by the manufacturer of certain luxury perfumery products offered for sale, promotion and advertising, on Amazon's online marketplace. In particular, the Court held that Amazon plays an active role when, as in the present case, it acts in such a way that consumers may consider that there is a link between Amazon and the companies producing the products sold on the platform. Such a link can be deemed to exist when Amazon operates a customer service for third-party sales listings, which constitutes the only service available to the customer for interfacing with the seller or is responsible for a promotional activity also through advertisements on third-party websites.

or take other measures aimed at detecting, identifying and removing, or disabling access to, illegal content.

Acting diligently and in good faith is for the Digital Services Act a non-discriminatory act. This is confirmed by whereas 26 of the Digital Services Act which specifies that non-discrimination in the conduct of business becomes a parameter for assessing whether intermediary service providers act diligently and in good faith.[62]

Whereas 26 and the Article 7 of the Digital Services Act further provide that the mere fact that providers take measures, in good faith, to comply with the requirements of European Union law, including those set out in the Digital Services Act as regards the implementation of their terms and conditions, should not render unavailable the exemptions from liability.

In this regard, it should be noted that whereas 26 itself specifies that this rule does not imply, however, that the provider may necessarily rely on the liability exemptions.[63]

Consequently, carrying out voluntary investigations does not preclude neutrality, but does not necessarily guarantee exemption of liability. This could lead to hosting services either being discouraged from taking voluntary measures or being very strict in removing content to the detriment of the protection of freedom of expression.[64]

Certainly, as far as it is relevant here, a lender who acts in a discriminatory manner is not a lender acting in good faith and in a diligent manner and therefore cannot benefit from the exemption from liability.

A significant example of the trend of classifying active hosting is the Directive 2019/790/EU on copyright and related rights in the Digital Single Market.[65] The

---

[62] See Kuczerawy (2021), p. 5, where we read that ‹‹whereas 25 concludes that the rule on determination of neutrality does not imply "that the provider can necessarily rely thereon". In other words, taking voluntary actions in good faith neither guarantees not precludes neutrality. The possibility of losing immunity still exists. Could that be the case when the host undertakes voluntary actions but not particularly successful ones? Would unsuccessful voluntary actions be considered as not undertaken in a "diligent manner"? Could it discourage hosts from taking onetime voluntary decisions in particular cases if no coherent framework for "diligence" is in place?».

[63] See Buri van Hoboken (2021).

[64] See whereas 41 of Com 2020 (825) final. Regarding the role of registering on social networks see Perlingieri (2014), p. 66. Wielsch (2019), p. 197 states that in the context of such social constitutions, protection of freedom is primarily accomplished through developing standards of due process for private regulation. In particular, the author considers that the protection of fundamental rights takes effect to a great extend through the construction of procedures.

[65] The Directive on copyright and related rights in the Digital Single Market does not refer, in general, to providers of information society services but to a particular category of provider, namely the so-called content sharing providers, identified as providers of an information society service of which the main or one of the main purposes is to store and give the public access to a large amount of copyright-protected works or other protected subject matter uploaded by its users, which it organises and promotes for profit-making purposes. See Ghidini (2018), Pojaghi (2018), p. 445, Musso (2018), p. 471. Critical of the choices made in the directive is Quintais (2020). The author states that ‹‹despite some positive aspects, the Directive includes multiple problematic provisions, including the controversial new right for press publishers and the new liability regime for content-sharing platforms. On balance, the Directive denotes a normative preference for private ordering

relationship between the Digital Services Act and the European Union copyright acquis can be interesting for several profiles.[66]

According to Article 17(4) of the Directive 2019/790/EU, online content–sharing service providers are exempt from liability if they can demonstrate that they have made best efforts to obtain an authorisation and made, in accordance with high industry standards of professional diligence, best efforts to ensure the unavailability of specific works and other subject matter for which the rightholders have provided the service providers with the relevant and necessary information.[67] This provision is not easy to coordinate with E–Commerce Directive and the idea of a provider playing a passive role.[68] Here too, as in Article 31 of the Digital Services Act, best efforts is required in the performance of the provider's activity.[69]

There is, therefore, at the European level, greater attention to cases in which the digital service intermediary performs such an activity that he cannot be considered a mere transmitter of other people's information and, as such, exempt from liability.[70]

---

over public choice in EU copyright law and lacks adequate safeguards for users. It is also a complex text with multiple ambiguities, which will likely fail to promote the desired harmonization and legal certainty in this area››.

[66] Peukert et al. (2022).

[67] Riccio (2022), p. 1032, Dusollier (2020), p. 979, states the legislative text aims at adapting copyright to the digital world, remedying some gaps and uncompensated uses of works and other subject matter, and enhancing some valuable uses through new or reaffirmed exceptions. On intermediaries as key actors in copyright enforcement, see Burri, Zihlmann (2021). Geiger and Jütte (2021), p. 517, are critical of Article 17 of the Directive 2019/790/EU, believing it to be the result of hard-fought compromises during the elaboration of the Directive which led to the adoption of a long provision with complicated wording and full of internal contradictions.

[68] See Moscon (2020), p. 980. The author asserts that new legal provisions concerning online intermediaries took a first steptoward a real paradigm shift regarding online intermediaries and their liability for third-party infringements. Article 17 of the Directive on Copyright in the Digital Single Market enacts a direct liability system for online content-sharing services providers copyright infringements committed by their users. Therefore, with specific regard to copyright infringement, Art. 17 derogates from the safe harbour regime of the E-Commerce Directive and opens the way to increased accountability and enhanced liability of online intermediaries. See Court of Justice of the European Union, in Case C-401/19, Poland v. the European Parliament and the European Council. The Court dismisses that action brought by Poland. According to the Court, the obligation, on online content-sharing service providers, to review, prior to its dissemination to the public, the content that users wish to upload to their platforms, resulting from the specific liability regime established in the Directive, has been accompanied by appropriate safeguards by the European Union legislature in order to ensure respect for the right to freedom of expression and information of the users of those services, and a fair balance between that right, on the one hand, and the right to intellectual property, on the other. On this judgment see Grossi (2022), p. 302.

[69] More precisely, the Digital Services Act refers to particular efforts, but as in the Directive 2019/790/EU, the a technical character of the term "efforts" cannot but be pointed out. See, for example, whereas 46 states that providers of intermediary services that are primarily directed at minors, for example through the design or marketing of the service, or which are used predominantly by minors, should make particular efforts to render the explanation of their terms and conditions easily understandable to minors. In the same terms also whereas 73 and (74).

[70] Rott (2023), p. 1039. He argues that until now, online platforms are by and large exempt from liability for unlawful third-party content, and they exempt any liability for such content in the standard terms of their contracts with users. The Digital Services Act introduces new duties of

For the purposes of non–discrimination protection, greater responsibility of providers, as well as the equalisation of discriminatory content with illegal content and more detailed notice and takedown mechanisms are certainly important steps forward that can be taken thanks to the Digital Services Act. However, we still need to go a step further, because to effectively protect against the risk of discrimination, it would also be necessary for platforms to reduce the initial differences between users with different backgrounds and to help users belonging to discriminated groups to interact on the platforms. Strongly discriminatory is, for example, the fact that most platforms only allow users to provide a rating after they have made a transaction through the platform.

A recent study of a Dutch motorcycle-sharing platform is illustrative, and it was found that there are very few renters belonging to ethnic minorities. Reliability indicators are affected by demographic information and those belonging to certain ethnic minorities actually have fewer opportunities to interact with the potential counterpart of the service. This leads to a lower rating possibility and, consequently, to a lower possibility of a positive rating, which, in turn, leads to a further decrease in their possibility of participating in future interactions.[71]

This is even more worrying if one considers that it has been shown that rating systems may not be able to overcome the inequalities caused by discriminatory tendencies.[72] Even if ethnic minority users manage to compensate their initial disadvantage with a good reputation, the rating system as a whole maintains the disadvantage of ethnic minority tenants.

It is necessary, at this point, to go into the specifics of some examples of possible discrimination in the digital market. The following chapter is devoted to these aspects.

---

online platforms, some of which relate to their dealings with information provided by third parties to consumers and with illegal content. The author explores whether those new duties, or rather their breach, can nevertheless trigger civil liability of online platforms towards victims of unlawful third-party content, where harm could have been avoided if the online platform had complied with its duties, and it presents examples where this seems possible. Compare, on the point, Rolph (2021), p. 122.

[71] Kas et al. (2022), p. 1912.

[72] Kas (2022), p. 1925. They assert that the emphasis on an experience of "personal contact" through revealing personal details by peer-to-peer market platforms has the unintended consequence of opening the door to discrimination based on precisely this personal information, and our results indicate that the effectiveness of "institutional" solutions as implemented by platforms to mitigate such discrimination may be limited. Practitioners should be aware of the possibility that reputation systems may exacerbate rather than reduce inequalities between users with different backrounds. While reputation systems may improve the chances for some individuals to participate on the platform, they may, as an unintended consequence, reduce the chances for others.

References

Achleitner RA (2021) Der künftige Digital Services Act der EU: Neue Pflichten und Verantwortlichkeiten für Anbieter digitaler Dienste. Zeitschrift für Energie und Technikrecht 1:1–10

Achleitner RA (2023) Der Digital Services Act als risikobasierte Regulierung – Zu den Auswirkungen des risikobasierten Ansatzes des DSA auf Desinformation und den Grundrechtsschutz. Medien Und Recht International 4:114–121

Allen A, Stockhem O (2022) A Series on the EU Digital Services Act: tackling illegal content online. https://cdt.org/insights/a-series-on-the-eu-digital-services-act-tackling-illegal-content-online. Accessed 19 Juli 2023

Bawack RE, Wamba SF, Carillo KDA, Akter S (2022) Artificial intelligence in e-commerce: a bibliometric study and literature review. Electron Markets 32:297–338

Bertelli G, Corsi M (2020) Amazon è responsabile per i danni causati dalla merce venduta in California. Analisi della sentenza ed applicabilità al contesto normativo europeo. www.iusinitinere.it. Accessed 19 Juli 2023

Bogani R, Schafer B (2022) Artificial intelligence and children's rights. In: Ienca M, Pollicino O, Liguori L, Stefanini E, Andorno R (eds.) The Cambridge handbook of information technology, life sciences and human rights. Cambridge University Press, Cambridge, pp 215–230

Buri I, van Hoboken J (2021) The Digital Services Act (DSA) proposal: a critical overview. Published as part of the DSA Observatory, a research project by the Institute for Information Law (IViR) at the Faculty of Law University of Amsterdam, with the support of Open Society Foundation. https://dsa-observatory.eu/wp-content/uploads/2021/11/Buri-Van-Hoboken-DSA-discussion-paper-Version-28_10_21.pdf. Accessed 10 Juli 2023

Busch C (2020) The P2B Regulation (EU) 2019/1150: towards a "procedural turn" in EU platform regulation? J Eur Consumer Market Law 4:133–134

Caggiano G (2021) Il contrasto alla disinformazione tra nuovi obblighi delle piattaforme online e tutela dei diritti fondamentali nel quadro del Digital Service Act e della coregolamentazione. Annali AISDUE 1:45–71

Charisi V, Chaudron S, Di Gioia R, Vuorikiari R, Escobar–Planas M, Sanchez I, Gomez E (2022), Artificial intelligence and the rights of the child. In: Towards an integrated agenda for research and policy. UR 31048 EN, Publications Office of the European Union, Luxembourg. https://doi.org/10.2760/012329, JRC127564

Clarizia R (2020) Mercato, persona, intelligenza artificiale, quale futuro? Jus Civile 3:687–723

Clarke O (2022) Liability of online platforms under the EU's proposed Digital Services Act. https://www.osborneclarke.com. Accessed 19 Juli 2023

D'Alfonso G (2020) Verso una maggiore responsabilizzazione dell'hosting provider tra interpretazione evolutiva della disciplina vigente, innovazioni legislative e prospettive de jure condendo. https://www.federalismi.it. Accessed 10 Juli 2023

De Franceschi A (2018) Uber Spain and the "identity crisis" of online platforms. J Eur Consumer Market Law 7:1–4

Dusollier S (2020) The 2019 directive on copyright in the digital single market: some progress, a few bad choices, and an overall failed ambition. Common Market Law Rev 4:979–1030

Eecke PV (2011) Online service providers and liability: a plea for a balanced approach. Common Market Law Rev 48:1455–1502

Eifert M, Metzger A, Schweitzer H, Wagner G (2021) Taming the giants: the DMA/DSA package. Common Market Law Rev 58:987–1028

Finocchiaro G (2023) Diritto di internet. Zanichelli, Bologna

Geiger C, Jütte BJ (2021) Platform liability under Article 17 of the copyright in the digital single market directive, automated filtering and fundamental rights: an impossible match. J Eur Int IP Law 70:3–52

Genç-Gelgeç B (2022) Regulating digital platforms: will the DSA correct its predecessor's deficiencies? Croatian Yearbook Eur Law Policy 18:25–60

Ghidini G (2018) Rethinking intellectual property: balancing conflicts of interest in the constitutional paradigm. Edward Elgar Publishing. Cheltenam, Northampton
Grisi G (2020) Le magnifiche sorti progressive del turismo 5.0. Europa e diritto privato 2:475–485
Grossi F (2022) La sentenza della Corte di Giustizia dell'Unione europea del 26 aprile 2022 sul ricorso proposto dalla Polonia avverso alcune disposizioni dell'art. 17 della direttiva (UE) 2019/790 sul copyright nel mercato unico digitale (Causa C–401/19). Persona e Mercato. Osservatorio OGID 2:302–305
Guibault L, Helberger N, Loos M, Mak C, Pessers L, van der Sloot B (2012), Digital consumers and the law: towards a cohesive European framework. Kluwer law International, Alphen aan den Rijn
Hiwatashi Dos Santos G (2020) A "new deal for consumers"? The European regulatory framework for online search queries and rankings under the omnibus directive (Directive (EU) 2019/2161). Anuário Do Nova Consumer Lab 2:65–89
Hong M (2022) Regulating hate speech and disinformation online while protecting freedom of speech as an equal and positive right—Comparing the Fundamental Rights' Frameworks in Germany, Europe and the United States. J Media Law 14:1–23
Kas J, Corten R, Van de Rijt A (2022) The role of reputation systems in digital discrimination. Soc Econ Rev 4:1905–1932
Kohl U (2022) Platform regulation of hate speech—A transatlantic speech compromise? J Media Law 14:25–49
Korpisaari P (2022) From Delfi to Sanchez – when can an online communication platform be responsible for third–party comments? an analysis of the practice of the ECtHR and some reflections on the digital services act. J Media Law 14:352–377
Kuczerawy A (2021) The Good Samaritan that wasn't: voluntary monitoring under the (draft) Digital Services Act. https://www.law.kuleuven.be. Accessed 19 Juli 2023
Lahe J, Turk K (2012) The Web Host's privilege of limited liability: its application to operators of commentary rooms. Eur Rev Private Law 20:447–472
Lasorella G (2021) Audizione del Presidente dell'autorità per le garanzie nelle comunicazioni. https://d110erj175o600.cloudfront.net. Accessed 19 Juli 2023
Lodder AR, Carvalho JM (2022) Online Platforms: towards an information tsunami with new requirements on moderation, ranking, and traceability. Eur Bus Law Rev 33:537–556
Martinelli S (2023) I contratti della platform economy. Ruoli e responsabilità delle piattaforme. Giappichelli, Turin
Maxwell W (2022) Applying Net neutrality rules to social media content moderation systems. Annales des Mines – Enjeux Numérique 1:90–98
Moscon V (2020) Free circulation of information and online intermediaries—Replacing one "Value Gap" with another. Int Rev Intellect Property Competition Law 51:977–982
Musso A (2018) L'impatto dell'ambiente digitale su modelli e categorie dei diritti d'autore o connessi. Rivista trimestrale di diritto e procedure civile 2:471–508
Ortolani P (2022) If you build it, they will come. The DSA's "procedure before substance" approach. https://verfassungsblog.de/dsa-build-it. Accessed 19 April 2023
Palmieri A (2019) Profili giuridici delle piattaforme digitali. La tutela degli utenti commerciali e dei titolari di siti web aziendali. Giappichelli, Turin
Panetta R (2019) Il ruolo dell'internet service provider e i profili di responsabilità civile. Responsabilità civile e previdenza 3:1017–1035
Perlingieri C (2014) Profili civilistici dei social networks. ESI, Naples
Petruso R (2018) Responsabilità delle piattaforme online, oscuramento di siti web e libertà di espressione nella giurisprudenza della Corte europea dei diritti dell'Uomo. Diritto dell'informazione e dell'informatica 3:511–588
Peukert A, Husovec M, Kretschmer M, Mezei P, Quintais JP (2022) European Copyright Society—Comment on copyright and the digital services act proposal. https://www.ivir.nl/publicaties/download/IIC_2022.pdf. Accessed 20 June 2023

Piraino F (2020) Il commercio elettronico- In: Pasquino T, Rizzo A, Tescaro M (eds) Questioni attuali in tema di commercio elettronico. ESI, Naples
Pojaghi A (2018) Il diritto d'autore nel mercato unico digitale. Iustitia 4:441–449
Price L (2021) Platform responsibility for online harms: towards a duty of care for online hazards. J Media Law 13:1–24
Petruso R (2022) Danno da prodotto difettoso e responsabilità delle piattaforme di e-commerce: uno sguardo oltreoceano. Persona e Mercato 1:59–78
Quintais J (2020) The new copyright in the digital single market directive: a critical look. Eur Intellect Prop Rev 42:28–41
Resta G (2019) Governare l'innovazione tecnologica: decisioni algoritmiche, diritti digitali e principio di uguaglianza. Politica Del Diritto 50:199–236
Riccio GM (2022) Responsabilità delle piattaforme e sistemi di filtraggio: quale destino per la normativa italiana sul diritto d'autore? Nuova giurisprudenza civile commentata 38:1032–1037
Rolph D (2021) Liability for third party comments on social media pages. J Media Law 13:122–134
Rott P (2023) New liability of online marketplaces under the digital services act? Eur Rev Private Law 6:1039–1058
Salanitro U (2020) Intelligenza artificiale e responsabilità: la strategia della Commissione europea. Rivista di diritto civile 6:1246–1276
Stark B, Stegmann D, Jürgens P, Magin M (2020) Are algorithms a threat to democracy? The rise of intermediaries: a challenge for public discourse. https://algorithmwatch.org. Accessed 21 Juli 2023
Tereszkiewicz P (2018) Digital platforms: regulation and liability in the EU law. Eur Rev Private Law 26:903–920
Tommasi S (2020) The 'New Deal' for consumers: towards more effective protection? Eur Rev Private Law 28:311–332
Tommasi S (2021) Verso il Digital Services Act: la Proposta di Regolamento sul "mercato unico dei servizi digitali" del 15.12.202. Persona e Mercato. Osservatorio OGID 1:213–217
Tommasi S (2022a) Approvato il "Digital Services Act": Regolamento (UE) 2022/2065 del 19.10.2022 relativo a un mercato unico dei servizi digitali e che modifica la direttiva 2000/31/CE. Persona e Mercato. Osservatorio OGID 4:698–701
Tommasi S (2022b) The liability of internet service providers in the proposed digital services act. Eur Rev Private Law 29:925–944
Trengove M, Kazim E, Almeida D, Hillard A, Zannone S, Lomas E (2022) A critical review of the Online Safety Bill. https://doi.org/10.1016/j.patter.2022.100544
Ullrich C (2021) Unlawful Content online, Towards a new regulatory framework for online platforms. Luxemburger Juristische Studien, Baden–Baden
Versaci G (2021) Le tutele a favore del consumatore digitale nella "Direttiva omnibus." Persona e Mercato 3:583–595
Wielsch D (2019) Private law regulation of digital intermediaries. Eur Rev Private Law 27:197–220
Zihlmann Z (2021) Intermediaries' liability in light of the recent EU copyright reform. Ind J Intellect Property Law 12:1–24

Chapter 3
Digital Services and Algorithmic Discrimination

Abstract This chapter deals specifically with the contribution that the Digital Services Act can make in protecting against algorithmic discrimination and, in particular, against the forms of discrimination by online platforms in advertising and dynamic pricing activities. Individuals may be vulnerable or disadvantaged in their use of online services because of any ground such as sex, race, colour, ethnic or social origin, genetic features, language, religion or belief, political or any other opinion, membership of a national minority, property, birth, disability, age or sexual orientation. The effects of such discrimination are amplified in the digital marketplace also for the use of algorithms by digital service providers. Algorithms work from a pre-selection of historical data and make statistical calculations for predictive purposes, but often also for decision-making or manipulative purposes. The decision taken statistically, even if based on a functioning algorithm, might be incorrect, especially in individual cases. Statistics, in fact, provide indications that are even more reliable when they are calibrated on an overall and not just a local effect.

Keywords Algorithmic discrimination · Online advertising · Online platforms · Dynamic pricing

3.1 Algorithmic Discrimination: Premise

Groups or individuals may be vulnerable or disadvantaged in their use of online services because of any ground such as sex, race, colour, ethnic or social origin, genetic features, language, religion or belief, political or any other opinion, membership of a national minority, property, birth, disability, age or sexual orientation.[1] The effects of such discrimination are amplified in the digital marketplace.[2]

On the one hand, the right not to be discriminated against is not indifferent to how one interacts with algorithms and artificial intelligence systems. On the other hand,

[1] On the prohibition of discrimination in Article 21 of the European Union Charter of Fundamental Rights, see Peers et al. (2021), p. 613.

[2] See Zuiderveen Borgesius (2020), p. 2. These are old issues that need to be treated with a new urgency. In this sense see Pezzoli and Tonazzi (2019), p. 201.

S. Tommasi, *The Risk of Discrimination in the Digital Market*,
SpringerBriefs in Law, https://doi.org/10.1007/978-3-031-43640-6_3

‹‹algorithmic discrimination can "spread" at a wider scale and a much quicker pace than "human" discrimination since algorithms both speed up and scale up decision making››.[3]

Discovering unknown correlations lies in the very nature of algorithms, which are therefore able to discriminate in new ways. The latter, in fact, refer to pre-established discriminating criteria.[4]

The ontological data correlation and combination skills of the algorithms used by online intermediary service providers make cases of intersectional discrimination even more frequent. These are forms of discrimination determined by the synergy of several discriminatory factors. Consequently, effective protection is only possible by analysing these factors in combination, rather than considering them individually.[5]

The case of additive discrimination is different when a subject can be discriminated against on several grounds, each with its own independent incidence and capable of being proven independently of the other discriminating factors.[6]

It is well known that algorithms are not neutral tools based on objective calculations, but feed on data provided by human beings. The supposed neutrality of technology can conceal the perpetuation of social inequalities and discriminatory stereotypes, despite the efforts made over the years to eliminate them.[7]

The supposed neutrality of technology may also distract from the fact that artificial intelligence is shaped by economic, political, cultural and historical forces.[8]

---

[3] Gerards and Xenidis (2021), p. 8. The authors say, p. 7, that the increasing use of algorithms in Europe poses specific risks in terms of fundamental rights protection and in particular in terms of equality and non-discrimination. See also Timmis et al. (2015), p. 1.

[4] See Xenidis (2018), p. 53, where the authors highlight ‹‹a gap between the empirically demonstrated problems posed by multiple discrimination and the patchy protection offered by EU law››.

[5] With reference to the problems posed by the fact that there is no new category of discrimination resulting from the combination of certain grounds, such as sexual orientation and age, see, e.g., Case C-443/15, David L. Parris v. Trinity College Dublin and Others. https://eurlex.europa.eu.

[6] See Wójcik (2022), p. 94. It also gives some significant examples. We read, in fact, that ‹‹additive discrimination occurs when patients are simultaneously discriminated against on several grounds-such as race, ethnicity, religion or belief, sex, sexual orientation, age, or disability—and when each type of discrimination can be proven independently. For example, a disabled gay person can face discriminatory treatment in accessing health care because of both their disability and their sexual orientation. Intersectional discrimination, on the other hand, is not based on the additive character of discrimination grounds but rather on their unique synergy. For example, the experience of ethnic minority women who access reproductive health care is qualitatively different both from the experience of ethnic minority men and from the experience of white women››.

[7] Wójcik (2022), p. 93. The author says that the thesis of the neutrality of technology overlooks the fact that the concrete role of a technology derives first and foremost from its form and its specific modes of use, which help to define its social meaning and scope. There are effects that are produced by the mere fact that one chooses to use a given technology. On the so-called net neutrality as a concept still in search of an unambiguous definition and underlying different problems, see Fachechi (2017), Airoldi and Gambetta (2018), p. 29, D'Aloia (2019), p. 16, Calders and Žliobaitė (2013), p. 43.

[8] See Crawford (2021).

Using a data set that is sufficiently representative and does not reflect pre-existing social and cultural expectations is not easy, as the configuration of the data set always implies a choice.[9]

If historical distortions remain, algorithms inevitably exacerbate marginalisation.[10] The unequal conditions of the past are reflected in the prognostic process.[11] The latter inevitably considers what happened in the past. This poses no problem when natural occurrences, such as the course of disturbances for weather forecasting purposes, are considered. The same cannot be said, however, when predictive techniques concern human beings and social processes.[12]

Algorithms work from a pre-selection of historical data and make statistical calculations for predictive purposes, but often also for decision-making or manipulative purposes.[13]

The decision taken statistically, even based on a functioning algorithm, might be incorrect, especially in individual cases.[14] Statistics, in fact, provide indications that are even more reliable when they are calibrated on an overall and not just a local effect.[15] Potentially detrimental effects may occur at any time when the algorithm is operating, not only at the time of data collection, but also in the organisation, aggregation, algorithmic design, interpretation, prediction and visualisation of the data.[16]

---

[9] Bucci (2021).

[10] See Ethics Guidelines for Trustworthy Artificial Intelligence of 8 April 2019, p. 24, where it is emphasised that algorithmic discrimination could be counteracted by putting in place oversight processes to analyse and address the system's purpose, constraints, requirements and decisions in a clear and transparent manner. Moreover, hiring from diverse backgrounds, cultures and disciplines can ensure diversity of opinions and should be encouraged. With reference to the Ethics Guidelines for Trustworthy Artificial Intelligence, see Floridi (2019), p. 261, Floridi (2021), p. 19, Zuiderveen Borgesius (2018, 2019), Fazio (2023), p. 82.

[11] The etymology of the word "statistics" refers to the "state", "situation or condition of a thing" situation that has occurred in the past. See Caporale (1876), p. 45.

[12] Resta (2019), p. 216. Consider the case of the so-called feedback-loop bias, which occurs if the data reflect systemic bias toward different groups, existing patterns of discrimination can be entrenched in the algorithm. On this point compare Wójcik (2022), p. 98.

[13] On how in automated algorithmic decisions the vision of the past conditions the future, see Falletti (2022), p. 291.

[14] Gini (1939). The author states that the calculus of probability and statistics by means of the calculus of probability, even when applied to masses of cases, can never lead to certain conclusions, but only to probable conclusions. They can legitimise doubts to a greater or lesser degree—and this is certainly a useful function—but they can never definitively resolve them. They can provide not "texts of significance" but "elements of suspicion".

[15] About the limits of statistics in dealing with individual behaviour see Israel (2015).

[16] With reference to discrimination caused by artificial intelligence systems, at the Process Level and at the Classification Level, see Daelman and Yordanova (2023), p. 134, Koen and Shepherd (2017), p. 211. An interesting experiment is the European Travel Information and Authorisation System (ETIAS). This is an EU information technology system, planned to become operational in May 2023, that will provide travel authorisation to visa-exempt third-country nationals using a profiling algorithm. On this point, see Derave et al. (2022), p. 389.

Biases may also be the consequence of the tool used to collect the data. One thinks of the distortions produced using an unsuitable data collection instrument in the 2011 experiment conducted in the city of Boston. In this case, an artificial intelligence system was used to collect information on the presence of serious irregularities in the road surface of the city's road network through the smartphones of motorists. In the most deprived neighbourhoods, where the roads were generally in the worst condition, but the inhabitants were largely without smartphones, the reports sent were lower than those recorded in the neighbourhoods inhabited by the better-off classes, with the result that the system prioritised maintenance work in neighbourhoods with better quality roads.[17]

Algorithms create real traps, often mostly invisible.[18] This is confirmed by the numerous examples of algorithmic discrimination.

3.2 Algorithms and New Forms of Discrimination

Examples of algorithmic discrimination can be many and affect all aspects of a person's life, from the most futile to the most essential.[19]

A recent example, that took place in Italy, concerns the algorithm known as "Frank", which adopts a rider profiling system based on the two parameters of reliability and participation in the booked work session. The algorithm treated absence from work for trivial reasons and absence resulting from the exercise of constitutional rights, such as the right to strike or the right to health, in the same way. Since the platform did not know and did not want to know the reasons for the rider's non-participation in the booked session, it effectively discriminated against those who were justifiably absent, significantly reducing their future opportunities to access work.[20]

Also famous is the case of the software called Correctional Offender Management Profiling for Alternative Sanctions, known as Compass, used in America to predict the risk of recidivism of subjects undergoing criminal proceedings, but found to be discriminatory. It has been shown, in fact, that African American prisoners, with the same criminal profile, tend to be classified as high risk, much more frequently than their white counterparts, due to the presence of systematic prejudice against black people.[21]

---

[17] Zuiderveen Borgesius (2018), p. 19, Zuddas (2020), p. 10.

[18] Comopare Fry (2018), Simoncini (2019), p. 84, Simoncini and Suweis (2019), p. 87, Gilman (2020), Pisani (2023), p. 42.

[19] Longo and Scorza (2020).

[20] https://www.algoritmolegal.com/wp-content/uploads/2021/01/Sentencia-Bologna-Italia-Deliveroo-dic-2020-Original-italiano.pdf.

[21] Broussard (2019), p. 98, Airoldi (2020), p. 111. See COM (2020) 65 final, cit., p. 11 where it reads that certain artificial intelligence algorithms, when exploited for predicting criminal recidivism, can display gender and racial bias, demonstrating different recidivism prediction probability for women vs men or for nationals versus foreigners. On this point, please refer to Tolan et al. (2019).

With specific reference to gender equality, one thinks, for instance, of the use of artificial intelligence tools to develop voice assistants. In particular, one observes how such voice assistants are designed to be at the complete disposal of the owner and are rarely built with male features but, on the contrary, have women's voices and names, thus reinforcing long-standing forms of inequality.[22]

Equally discriminatory can be, as text mining studies have shown, the association of words with stereotypes. For example, if I type "she is an engineer, he is a teacher" into Google Translator and translate it into gender-neutral Turkish and then back into English, the translation gives us "He is an engineer, she is a teacher".[23]

The risks of gender discrimination linked to the increasing use of algorithms are known to the European Commission, which highlights them, for instance, in the recent Gender Equality Strategy 2020–2025, where it points out that algorithms and related machine learning, if not sufficiently transparent and robust, risk reproducing, amplifying or contributing to gender biases that programmers may not be aware of or that are the result of a specific selection of data.[24]

Then there is the danger of exclusion from goods or services due to the re-representation in the analysed data of a specific category of subjects, who, because they do not have access to the internet or are excluded from the formal economy, may be less "data-driven".[25]

In addition, for those who already face marginalisation or prejudice, the threats are also in the fact that ‹‹currently the loudest voices debating the potential dangers of superintelligence are affluent white men››.[26]

---

[22] Broussard (2019), p. 4. The author highlights cases of such algorithmically driven data failures that are specific to people of color and women and to underscore the structural ways that racism and sexism are fundamental to what she has coined algorithmic oppression.

[23] Shah (2018), Caliskan et al. (2017), p. 183. On gender discrimination caused by algorithms in the selection of a company's personnel see Martínez et al. (2021), p. 2. On this point see, Zuiderveen Borgesius (2018), p. 30.

[24] Some artificial intelligence programmes for facial analysis reflect biases related to gender and race, as they more easily identify the gender of light-skinned men while making more errors in determining the gender of darker-skinned women. On this topic compare Buolamwini and Gebru (2018), p. 77, Macchiavelli (2021), p. 381.

[25] Mattarella (2020) p. 674. For a comparison, in terms of classification accuracy, sensitivity, specificity, of seven real-world credit scoring datasets, see Tripathi et al. (2021), p. 217.

[26] Crawford (2016), p. 4. On the need to encourage the recruitment of personnel from different backgrounds, cultures and disciplines that can ensure diversity of opinion also in supervisory processes to clearly and transparently analyse and address the system's aims, constraints, requirements and decisions, see the Ethics Guidelines for Trustworthy Artificial Intelligence, cit., p. 24.

Algorithms, therefore, risk reinforcing existing patterns of disadvantage.[27] The examples, as seen, can be many.[28] Specifically, we will now go on to analyse the risk of discrimination in the digital market through advertising and dynamic prices.

3.3 Advertising Discrimination Through Online Platforms

Significant discriminatory risks may arise from online advertising either because it constitutes illegal content in itself or because of the discriminatory display of advertising. Faced with these possible discriminatory scenarios, the Digital Services Act provides, for the protection of service users, transparency obligations for platforms that display advertising on their online interfaces, with specific reference to the parameters used.

The provision of transparency obligations in the parameters used are not new, as evidenced by Regulation (EU) 2019/1150,[29] known as Online Platforms Regulation. This Regulation governs the contractual activity of the online intermediary service provider with its business users. This activity takes place at an earlier stage than the activity directly involving the consumer. Already at this stage, pursuant to Article 5 of the Online Platforms Regulation, providers of online intermediation services shall set out in their terms and conditions the main parameters determining ranking and the reasons for the relative importance of those main parameters as opposed to other parameters. Where the main parameters include the possibility to influence ranking against any direct or indirect remuneration paid by business users or corporate website users to the respective provider, that provider shall also set out a description of those possibilities and of the effects of such remuneration on ranking.[30]

---

[27] Barocas and Selbst (2016), p. 671.

[28] For other interesting examples, see Freire de Carvalho (2020), p. 1.

[29] Regulation (EU) 2019/1150 of the European Parliament and of the Council on promoting fairness and transparency for business users of online intermediation services, which applies to contractual relations between business users and online intermediary service providers. https://eur-lex.europa.eu. See also Guidelines on ranking transparency pursuant to Regulation (EU) 2019/1150 of the European Parliament and of the Council (2020/C 424/01). https://eur-lex.europa.eu.

[30] For in-depth and critical focus on what information should be communicated, how this information should be communicated, and at what moment, see Lodder and Morais Carvalho (2022), p. 537. About the role of Regulation (EU) 2019/1150 as the first step of the European Union's strategy to set new rules for the online platform economy, which will be soon expanded by the much anticipated "Digital Services Act Package" refer Busch (2020), p. 133.

The Digital Services Act is in line with the growing need for transparency of the parameters that lead to certain online search results,[31] imposing obligations in this direction also when regulating the activity of non-professional users.

In particular, the Digital Services Act provides for a double level of protection. One relates to non-systemic risks, for which protection is provided by Article 26 of the Digital Services Act, and the other refers to so-called systemic risks.

Concerning non-systemic risks, Article 26 of the Digital Services Act prescribes that providers of online platforms that present advertisements on their online interfaces shall ensure that, for each specific advertisement presented to each individual recipient, the recipients of the service are able to identify, in a clear, concise and unambiguous manner and in real time: that the information is an advertisement; the natural or legal person on whose behalf the advertisement is presented; the natural or legal person who paid for the advertisement if that person is different from the natural or legal person on whose behalf the advertisement is presented; meaningful information directly and easily accessible from the advertisement about the main parameters used to determine the recipient to whom the advertisement is presented and, where applicable, about how to change those parameters.

Article 26 of the Digital Services Act further confirms the difficulty of considering digital service intermediaries as always "passive" providers. This is also supported by Article 27 of the Digital Services Act, in addition to what has already been examined in chapter one with reference to Articles 30 and 31 of the Digital Services Act.

Article 27 of the Digital Services Act concerns recommendation systems that suggest, classify, and rank information based on algorithms, distinguishing it through text or other visual representations, or otherwise sorting the information provided by recipients.[32] These systems have a significant impact on the recipients' ability to retrieve and interact with online information and play an important role in amplifying

---

[31] On the transparency of parameters leading to certain online search results, see whereas 20 of Directive (Eu) 2019/2161 of the European Parliament and of the Council, as regards the better enforcement and modernisation of Union consumer protection rules, also known as the Omnibus Directive. https://eur-lex.europa.eu. The Omnibus Directive calls for an amendment of Annex I to Directive 2005/29/EC to make it clear that practices where a trader provides information to a consumer in the form of search results in response to the consumer's online search query without clearly disclosing any paid advertising or payment specifically for achieving higher ranking of products within the search results should be prohibited. When a trader has directly or indirectly paid the provider of the online search functionality for a higher ranking of a product within the search results, the provider of the online search functionality should inform consumers of that fact in a concise, easily accessible and intelligible form. Also explicit is whereas 21) of the Omnibus Directive where we read that the transparency requirements under that Regulation cover a broad range of online intermediaries, including online marketplaces, but they only apply between traders and online intermediaries. Similar transparency requirements should therefore be introduced in Directive 2005/29/EC to ensure adequate transparency towards the consumers, except in the case of providers of online search engines, which are already required by that Regulation to set out the main parameters which individually or collectively are most significant in determining ranking and the relative importance of those main parameters, by providing an easily and publicly available description, drafted in plain and intelligible language on the online search engines of those providers.

[32] See whereas 70 of the Digital Services Act.

certain messages and viral dissemination of information, thus not merely recommending content, but more precisely "curating" it. Several risks can be linked to the use of recommender systems: discriminatory treatment in the selection of content to be sent to recipients; the limitation of opportunities to receive commercial communications and alternative contractual offers; the impairment of the autonomy; the capturing of users' attention to induce them to remain active online.[33]

The version of the Digital Services Act prior to the amendments passed by the European Parliament on 20 January 2022 identified specific risks related to the use of recommender systems only with reference to the activities of very large platforms.

Instead, the amended version, through the introduction of Article 27, states that in general all online platforms that use recommender systems shall set out in their terms and conditions, in plain and intelligible language, the main parameters used in their recommender systems, as well as any options for the recipients of the service to modify or influence those main parameters.

The regulation of advertising systems used by very large online platforms is more articulated, due to the circumstance that their advertising recommendation, selection and display systems also influence systemic risks due to the potentially rapid and wide dissemination of illegal content.

Section 5 of the Digital Services Act provides, in fact, additional obligations for providers of very large online platforms and of very large online search engines to manage systemic risks. Providers of very large online platforms or of very large online search engines that present advertisements on their online interfaces shall compile and make publicly available in a specific section of their online interface, through a searchable and reliable tool that allows multicriteria queries and through application programming interfaces, a repository containing the accurate information referred to in Article 39(2) of the Digital Services Act, for the entire period during which they present an advertisement and until one year after the advertisement was presented for the last time on their online interfaces.[34]

---

[33] See Montinaro (2022), p. 348. The author focuses on the definition of recommender systems in the Digital Services Act and on some possible negative consequences connected to their use, pointing out that these consequences are not ineluctable corollaries of the use of this technology, but rather risks that the law is called upon to govern. Stark et al. (2020), p. 52, point out that «as the debate about the impact of algorithmic news recommenders on democracy is still an ongoing process, diversity-sensitive design as part of a possible solution should be considered. For such solutions to work, it should be clear that different perspectives on the democratic role of news recommenders imply different design principles for recommendation systems, i.e., an explicit normative conception of the democratic potential is critical. It may also become clear, that we need to work towards a coherent mix of appropriate government regulation, co-regulation, and platform-specific self-regulation to minimize the negative effects of the discussed threats». Hao et al. (2023), p. 1002, say that personality is a stable construction, which is associated with thoughts, emotions and behaviors of human. Any technology involved in understanding, analyzing and predicting human behaviors may benefit from personality recognition. Accurately recognizing the personality will contribute to the research of human–computer interaction. See Femia (2022), p. 135, Perlingieri (1990), p. 329, Di Ciommo (2003), p. 3, Kyaw et al. (2023), p. 1.

[34] Article 39(2) of the Digital Services Act states that the repository of the providers of very large online platforms or of very large online search engines that present advertisements on their online interfaces shall include at least all of the following information: the content of the advertisement,

The purpose of the above-mentioned articles is to facilitate vigilance and research into the risks arising from the distribution of online advertising, e.g., in relation to illegal advertising or manipulation and disinformation techniques that have real and foreseeable negative repercussions on public health, public safety, civic debate, political participation and equality.

A first form of protection against advertising discrimination is therefore linked to the possibility of knowing who decides to send an advertising message and based on which parameters.[35]

This is confirmed by Article 39(2) of the Digital Services Act, where it is specified that the repository shall include information so as to make it possible to understand whether the advertisement was intended to be presented specifically to one or more particular groups of recipients of the service and if so, the main parameters used for that purpose including where applicable the main parameters used to exclude one or more of such particular groups.

A protection entrusted only to the parameters of transparency of advertising may be a weak protection if one looks only at the relationship with the individual user of digital intermediary services. What is effective in practice is not so much the information received by the consumer or the individual consumer's knowledge of the general conditions of service. Experience shows that the average consumer does not even read those conditions, especially when online. Rather, the transparency of advertising parameters and recommendation systems must be a deterrent for platforms from engaging in unfair activity. Transparency, in this perspective, is important because without transparency as regulated in Articles 26, 27, 39 and 42 of the Digital Services Act, the supervisory authorities would not be able to valuate, for example, whether advertising is discriminatory or whether manipulative or misinformation techniques are used.

The Digital Services Act deals with sanctions mainly by setting a maximum amount of fines and the maximum amount of a periodic penalty payment, while repeating, rhetorically, that violations of the obligations laid down in this Regulation can be sanctioned in a manner that is effective, proportionate and dissuasive, taking

---

including the name of the product, service or brand and the subject matter of the advertisement; the natural or legal person on whose behalf the advertisement is presented; the natural or legal person who paid for the advertisement; the period during which the advertisement was presented; whether the advertisement was intended to be presented specifically to one or more particular groups of recipients of the service and if so, the main parameters used for that purpose including where applicable the main parameters used to exclude one or more of such particular groups; the commercial communications published on the very large online platforms and identified pursuant to Article 26(2) of the Digital Services Act; the total number of recipients of the service reached and, where applicable, aggregate numbers broken down by Member State for the group or groups of recipients that the advertisement specifically targeted.

[35] See, Schmidt and Stephens (2019), p. 144, where it is stated that «recognizing the existence and nature of algorithmic bias, as well as the risks associated with reliance on newly available data, is a necessary step to designing and implementing approaches to ensure that these algorithmic decision-making processes are as fair as possible. Unlawful bias arising from the use of algorithms can be evaluated and mitigated, but doing so requires a deep understanding of these new methods, data, and the contexts and domains in which they are being used». See Wachter (2020), p. 1.

into account the nature, gravity, recurrence and duration of the violation, in view of the public interest pursued, the scope and kind of activities carried out, as well as the economic capacity of the infringer.[36] Not least because the sanction regime of the Digital Services Act is limited, it is particularly important, also as a deterrent to misconduct, to consider digital service providers not as mere transmitters of other people's content, but as subjects responsible for the way in which they carry out their intermediation activities. In concrete terms, the most interesting aspects of the problems related to discriminatory advertising can be highlighted by analysing the phenomenon of dynamic pricing, to which the following remarks are devoted.

3.4 Dynamic Price and Discrimination

The phenomenon of dynamic pricing is linked to the growing practice of offering different prices for identical products depending on who the buyers are, where they are and the information collected about them, analysing the traces left by previous online searches and loyalty to a particular site.[37] It is the well-known phenomenon of the exploitation of the so-called "digital footprint" that can cause indirect discrimination.[38]

An example of price modulation according to what potential customers are willing to pay can be found in the insurance sector.[39]

The extent to which this can have discriminatory effects is clear to the Court of Justice of the European Union,[40] which has ruled that it is unlawful to allow differences in policy premiums depending on the impact of the gender factor in risk assessment,[41] considering accurate statistical data.[42]

---

[36] See Article 52 and Article 74 of the Digital Services Act.

[37] Li (2022), p. 2, states that terms such as "price discrimination" and "personalised pricing" may contain potential bias when used to describe online algorithmic pricing in the legal area, since not all personalised pricing is detrimental, and indeed not all algorithmic pricing is personalised. Compare Lynskey et al. (2021), p. 94, Federico (2021), p. 514, Tommasi (2021), p 112.

[38] Zuiderveen Borgesius (2020) p. 401.

[39] Porrini (2016), p. 47.

[40] See Court of Justice of the European Union 1 March 2011, C-236/09, Test-Achats, on the interpretation of the so-called Gender Directive, i.e. Directive 2004/113/EC of 13 December 2004 implementing the principle of equal treatment between men and women in the access to and supply of goods. https://eur-lex.europa.eu.

[41] Porrini (2000), p. 139. On discrimination affecting crucial opportunities, such as the ability to obtain credit, insurance, education, employment or even medical care, see Drozdz (2020), p. 152.

[42] Hacker (2018), p. 1186. See also Koldinská (2011), p. 1599, where it is stated that the area of gender equality is still a very dynamic and vital field in EU law, and that thanks to its long-lasting tradition it provides a very important source for legal argumentation and reflection. Muir (2013), p. 1231, points out that although EU equality law was initially designed to constrain public authorities in the context of the creation of a new legal order, it has progressively gained a second prominent function as a policy regulating inter-personal relationships.

The automated decision-making process for social scoring also raises numerous questions and highlights high risks of discrimination. The potentially discriminatory scope of such systems is recently recognised and reaffirmed by the General approach on the Artificial Intelligence Act of the Council of the European Union, 6 December 2022,[43] where it states that artificial intelligence systems providing social scoring of natural persons by public authorities or by private actors may lead to discriminatory outcomes and the exclusion of certain groups. They may violate the right to dignity and non-discrimination and the values of equality and justice. Such artificial intelligence systems evaluate or classify natural persons based on their social behaviour in multiple contexts or known or predicted personal or personality characteristics. The social score obtained from such artificial intelligence systems may lead to the detrimental or unfavourable treatment of natural persons or whole groups thereof in social contexts, which are unrelated to the context in which the data was originally generated or collected or to a detrimental treatment that is disproportionate or unjustified to the gravity of their social behaviour. Artificial intelligence systems entailing such unacceptable scoring practices should therefore be prohibited.

What is new is that the restriction on the use of artificial intelligence systems providing social scoring does not only apply to public authorities, as in the Proposed Artificial Intelligence Act of April 2021, but also to private actors.[44]

The General approach on the Artificial Intelligence Act of the Council of the European Union also considers the artificial intelligence systems used to evaluate the credit score or creditworthiness of natural persons. These are systems that should be classified as high-risk artificial intelligence systems, since they determine those persons' access to financial resources or essential services such as housing, electricity, and telecommunication services. Artificial intelligence systems used for this purpose may lead to discrimination of persons or groups and perpetuate historical patterns of discrimination, for example based on racial or ethnic origins, disabilities, age, sexual orientation, or create new forms of discriminatory impacts.[45]

[43] General approach on the Artificial Intelligence Act of the European Council of 6 December 2022. https://www.consilium.europa.eu.

[44] For a critique of the artificial intelligence systems providing social scoring in the Proposed Artificial Intelligence Act, see Ebers et al. (2021).

[45] General approach on the Artificial Intelligence Act of the European Council of 6 December 2022, p. 26.

Credit scoring[46] has consequences that are more serious, the more credit becomes a means of overcoming social problems, such as the purchase of a home, achieving the goals previously assigned to welfare.[47]

The difficulties are amplified by the circumstance that in the case of creditworthiness there is no objective criterion that establishes a definition of a creditworthy client, so that it ends up being referred to an assessment by the planner.[48]

It is also possible that the algorithm will reject the customer outright as an extra-positive target market, without performing the second-level analysis that inter-diaries usually perform to verify that the customer does not fall into the negative target market and that the product still meets the customer's needs. Among other things, the credit scoring criteria that are in fact followed today are questionable. It suffices to say that the traditional credit scoring models take salary and household composition as the main relevant variables, while alternative forms of credit scoring now consider data such as one's network of friends on Facebook or the time spent reading terms and conditions.[49]

The examples of algorithmic discrimination can be countless. Faced with this scenario, the solution certainly cannot be to halt technological development, which would not be possible, by the way.

One can, however, try to avoid both over-emphasis and over-confidence in algorithms, aiming to avert forms of discrimination concealed by alleged scientific bases.

We perceive technological development as both a promise and a threat,[50] because technological development is ambivalent by nature.[51]

---

[46] See Bajracharya et al. (2023). See COM (2020) 591 final, Communication from the Commission to the European Parliament, the Council, the European Economic and Social Committee and the Committee of the Regions on a Digital Finance Strategy for the EU. Also the European Parliament Resolution of 12 February 2020 on automated decision-making processes: ensuring consumer protection and free movement of goods and services (2019/2915(RSP)) only seems to hint at the discriminatory profiles, reducing them to those of Regulation (EU) 2018/302 of the European Parliament and of the Council of 28 February 2018 on addressing unjustified geo-blocking and other forms of discrimination based on customers' nationality, place of residence or place of establishment within the internal market.

[47] Mattarella (2020), p. 696.

[48] On the AppleCard algorithm, which has been shown to grant higher credit limits to men than to women despite the latter having higher credit scores, see Dastin (2022).

[49] Derave et al. (2022), p. 389.

[50] Rodotà (1997) p. 27, states that the image of a two-faced technology reappears, like the ancient God Janus. Facing us are "technologies of freedom" or "technologies of control?". On this point see Wilson (1988) Regarding the virtues and limits of technological innovations see Pardolesi and Davola (2019), p. 297. Wójcik (2022), p. 96, states that ‹‹on the one hand, AI offers solutions that can help tackle existing discriminatory practices. On the other, it can also create new patterns of discrimination, some of which are difficult to detect and address››.

[51] Timmis et al. (2015) p. 1 argue that whilst technology offers many potentially creative opportunities for innovation and for rethinking assessment purposes, there are also numerous risks and challenges. In particular, the authors highlight ethical concerns over social exclusion and new forms of digital dividedness.

Artificial intelligence systems for example, can be used both in a beneficial and in a harmful way. They can be used to offer us more personalised and qualitative services, yet they can also hamper our decisional autonomy. And while artificial intelligence systems can be used to enhance our security, they can also be deployed as a means of illegitimate surveillance and stifle our freedom. Artificial intelligence systems can be used to help us make more objective decisions, but they can also perpetuate and even exacerbate unfair biases.[52]

The risk of discrimination is not related to the algorithms or the technology itself, but to the use that humans decide to make of it.

Part of the doctrine has pointed out, for example, the advantages that consumers can gain from price personalisation.[53] This fact, on which one can also agree in the abstract, must be assessed bearing in mind that it is often based on the simplistic assumption that algorithms can perfectly reflect people's preferences. Indeed, it must be considered that personalisation is in any case based on data governance that depends on the quality and quantity of the data that feed the personalisation and the accuracy of the model used by the artificial intelligence system.[54] Moreover, algorithms approximate preferences that may have changed in practice, and if the only justification for the individualised rule is the presumed individual preference, the actual absence of that preference renders the rule arbitrary. In contrast, in a system of generalised legal rules, the justification for default rules goes beyond individual preferences.[55]

A further example of the ambivalent character of the use of algorithms can be drawn from the analysis of the problems concerning the risk of discrimination.

---

[52] Smuha (2019), p. 98.

[53] On the benefits that consumers can also get from price customisation see Porat and Strahilevitz (2021), p. 36. The authors argue that «in any event, it would be unwise to reject personalization solely on price-discrimination grounds». The authors themselves admit, p. 42, that «crude personalized default rules that are dependent on mere stereotypes are undesirable», but they believe that «granular personalized default rules based on hard data and sound science may be desirable». Maggiolino (2022) p. 112, says in recent times, there has been much discussion about pricing algorithms and the impact they might have on market dynamics. However, many of the fears raised are unfounded. The author points out that, on the one hand, personalized prices are unlikely to be an antitrust violation and, should this be the case, they are quite manageable using traditional antitrust tools. On the other hand, customized pricing, allows the dominant firm to extract a portion of the consumer surplus, but on the other hand, it also makes the dominant firm's products available to those consumers who could not buy them at the monopoly price.

[54] See Busch (2021), p. 192.

[55] In these terms Bender and Grigoleit (2021), p. 128. The authors note that «justificatory problems are exacerbated if one considers the possibility of approximation errors: Algorithms approximate preferences by analyzing available data and especially this data might not perfectly reflect what a person actually and currently wants. One may think, for instance, of a situation in which a person recently experienced a significant decrease in her degree of risk aversion and this development has not yet been reflected by the data on which the algorithm determines the degree of risk aversion». For a strong criticism see also Auer (2021) p. 145. The author states that «replacing hard discriminatory criteria by granular descriptions of consumer behavior thus amounts to a mere game with statistical correlations which inevitably leads back to the hard, constitutionally banned criteria such as gender and race».

Although, in fact, algorithms can discriminate, it is also true that they can help in terms of honouring the proof of discrimination, especially if the latter occurs in the digital sphere.[56] One considers the possibility of producing factual elements, also deduced from statistical data, capable of substantiating, in precise and concordant terms, the presumption of the existence of discriminatory acts, pacts or behaviour.[57]

That is, algorithms can offer opportunities to visualize detect and ultimately better correct discriminatory distortions, e.g., by detecting large-scale discriminatory job advertisements. An example may serve to clarify. Suppose an algorithmic system shows that a collection of archive photos contains gender stereotypes, «one interpretation is that the algorithmic system illustrates stereotyped behaviour that already exists. Hence, an algorithmic system could help to discover existing discrimination that would otherwise have remained hidden».[58]

These examples are of particular interest also because they can help to highlight the limits of non-discriminatory European legislation. The following chapter is devoted to these aspects.

References

Airoldi A (2020) Lo spettro dell'algoritmo e le scienze sociali. Prospettive critiche su macchine intelligenti e automazione delle disuguaglianze. Polis 34:111–128

Airoldi M, Gambetta D (2018) Sul mito della neutralità algoritmica. Lab's Quarter 4:25–47

Auer M (2021) Granular norms and the concept of law: a critique. In: Busch C, De Franceschi A (eds) Algorithmic regulation and personalized law. Verlag C.H, Beck oHG, München, pp 137–151

[56] Babu and Pushpa (2018), p. 213.

[57] See Court of Justice of the European Union, of 9 February 1999, Case C-167/97, Regina v Secretary of State for Employment, ex parte Nicole Seymour-Smith and Laura Perez. The Court states that:" in order to establish whether a rule adopted by a Member State, to the effect that protection against unfair dismissal applies only to employees who have been continuously employed for a minimum period of two years, has disparate effect as between men and women to such a degree as to amount to indirect discrimination for the purposes of Article 119 of the Treaty, the national court—which must determine, taking into account all the material legal and factual circumstances, the point in time at which the legality of a rule is to be assessed—must verify whether the statistics available indicate that a considerably smaller percentage of women than men is able to fulfil the requirement imposed by that measure. If that is the case, there is indirect sex discrimination, unless that measure is justified by objective factors unrelated to any discrimination based on sex. In that connection, it is for the Member State, as the author of the allegedly discriminatory rule, to show that the said rule reflects a legitimate aim of its social policy, that that aim is unrelated to any discrimination based on sex, and that it could reasonably consider that the means chosen were suitable for attaining that aim. Mere generalisations concerning the capacity of a specific measure to encourage recruitment are not enough to show that the aim of the disputed rule is unrelated to any discrimination based on sex or to provide evidence based on which it could reasonably be considered that the means chosen were suitable for achieving that aim". On artificial intelligence systems as a vehicle for equality, see Caterini (2020), Caterini (2022), p. 207.

[58] Zuiderveen Borgesius (2020), p. 5.

Babu MC, Pushpa S (2018) An efficient discrimination prevention and rule protection algorithms avoid direct and indirect data discrimination in web mining. Int J Intel Eng Syst 11:212–220
Bajracharya A, Khakurel U, Harvey B, Rawat DB (2023) Recent Advances in algorithmic biases and fairness in financial services: a survey. In: Arai K (eds) Proceedings of the future technologies conference (FTC) 2022. Springer, Cham. https://doi.org/10.1007/978-3-031-18461-1-53
Barocas S, Selbst AD (2016) Big data's disparate impact. Calif Law Rev 104:671–732
Bender PM, Grigoleit HC (2021) The law between generality and particularity. Chances and limits of personalized law. In: Busch C, De Franceschi A (eds) Algorithmic regulation and personalized law. Beck/Hart, München - Oxford - Baden-Baden, pp 115–136
Broussard M (2019) Artificial unintelligence. How computers misunderstand the world. The MIT Press, Cambridge
Bucci F (2021) Algoritmi e diritti umani: qual è il punto d'incontro? https://www.iusinitinere.it/algoritmi-e-diritti-umani-qual-e-il-punto-dincontro-34479. Accessed 20 May 2023
Buolamwini J, Gebru T (2018) Proceedings of the 1st Conference on fairness, accountability and transparency. Proc Mach Learn Res 81:77–91
Busch C (2020) The P2B regulation (EU) 2019/1150: towards a "procedural turn" in EU platform regulation? J Eur Consumer Market Law 4:133–134
Busch C (2021) Algorithmic regulation and (Im)perfect enforcement in the personalized economy. In: Busch C, De Franceschi A (eds) Algorithmic regulation and personalized Law. Verlag C.H, München, pp 279–291
Calders T, Žliobaitė I (2013) Why unbiased computational processes can lead to discriminative decision procedures. In: Bart C, Toon C, Schermer B, Zarsky T (eds) Discrimination and privacy in the information society: data mining and profiling in large databases. Springer, Berlin, Heidelberg, pp 43–57
Caliskan A, Bryson J, Narayanan A (2017) Semantics derived automatically from language corpora contain human-like biases. Science 356(6334):183–186
Camardi C (ed) (2022) La via europea per l'intelligenza artificiale. Atti del Convegno del Progetto Dottorale di Alta Formazione in Scienze Giuridiche Ca' Foscari Venezia, 25–26 novembre 2021, Wolters Kluwer, Cedam, Milan
Caporale G (1876) Corso di statisticaper l'insegnamento universitario e tecnico applicato ai dati ufficiali della statistica italiana dell'ultimo quinquiennio. Stabilimento Tipografico del comm. G. Nobile, Naples
Caterini E (2020) L'intelligenza artificiale "sostenibile" e il processo di socializzazione del diritto civile. ESI, Naples
Caterini E (2022) Artificial Intelligence, persona e soggetto. Tecnologie e Diritto 2:207–250
Crawford K (2016) Artificial intelligence's white guy problem. https://www.nytimes.com/2016/06/26/opinion/sunday/artificial-intelligences-white-guy-problem.html. Accessed 19 July 2023
Crawford K (2021) Atlas of AI. Power, politics and the planetary costs of artificial intelligence. Yale University Press, New Haven and London
D'Aloia A (2019) Il diritto verso "il mondo nuovo". Le sfide dell'Intelligenza Artificiale. Rivista di BioDiritto 1:3–31
Daelman C, Yordanova K (2023), AI through a human rights lens. The role of human rights in fulfilling AI's potential. In: De Bruyne J, Vanleenhove C (eds) Artificial intelligence and the law. Intersentia, Cambridge, pp 135–168
Dastin J (2022) Amazon scraps secret AI recruiting tool that showed bias against women. In: Kirsten M (ed) Ethics of data and analytics. CRC Press, Boca Raton, pp 296–300
Derave C, Genicot N, Hetmanska N (2022) The risks of trustworthy artificial intelligence: the case of the European travel information and authorisation system. Eur J Risk Regulat 13:389–420
Di Ciommo F (2003) Diritti della personalità tra media tradizionali e avvento di Internet. In Comandé G (ed) Persona e tutele giuridiche. Giappichelli, Turin, pp 1–45
Drozdz A (2020) Protection of natural persons with regard to automated individual decision-making in the GDPR. Wolters Kluwer, Netherlands

Ebers M, Hoch VRS, Rosenkranz F, Ruschemeier H, Steinrötter B, The European Commission's proposal for an artificial intelligence Act. A critical assessment by members of the robotics and AI law society. J 4:1–15. https://econpapers.repec.org/article/gamjjopen/v_3a4_3ay_3a2021_3ai_3a4_3ap_3a43-603_3ad_3a651448.htm. Accessed 30 June 2023

Fachechi A (2017) Net neutrality e discriminazioni arbitrarie. ESI, Naples

Falletti E (2022) Discriminazione algoritmica. Una prospettiva comparata. Giappichelli, Turin

Fazio E (2023) Intelligenza artificiale e diritti della persona. Esi, Naples

Federico A (2021) Equilibrio e contrattazione algoritmica. Rassegna di diritto civile 2:483–516

Femia P (2022) Tumulti contrattuali. Collettivo "fluido" nei social media, socializzazione sinallagmatica, reticolarità, azione contrattuale comune. In: Camardi C (ed) La via europea per l'intelligenza artificiale. Atti del Convegno del Progetto Dottorale di Alta Formazione in Scienze Giuridiche Ca' Foscari Venezia, 25–26 Novembre 2021, Wolters Kluwer–Cedam, Milan, pp 99–145

Floridi L (2019) Establishing the rules for building trustworthy AI. Nat Mach Intell 1:1–2

Floridi L (eds) (2021) Ethics, governance, and policies in artificial intelligence. Philosophical studies series. Springer, Cham

Freire de Carvalho B (2020) Discriminação algorítmica e transparência na lei geral de proteção de dados pessoais. Revista de Direito e as Novas Tecnologias. https://bd.tjdft.jus.br/jspui/handle/tjdft/49512. Accessed 20 Juli 2023

Fry H (2018) Hello world: how to be human in the age of the machine. Transworld Penguin, London

Gerards J, Xenidis R (2021) Algorithmic discrimination in Europe: challenges and opportunities for gender equality and non discrimination law. European Commission, Directorate-General for Justice and Consumers. Publications Office. https://data.europa.eu/doi/10.2838/544956

Gilman ME (2020) Poverty lawgorithms: a poverty lawyer's guide to fighting automated decision-making harms on low-income communities. Data & Society. https://ssrn.com/abstract=3699650. Accessed 30 May 2023

Gini C (1939) I pericoli della Statistica. http://blog.petiteplaisance.it/wp-content/uploads/2018/01/04-Corrado-Gini-I-pericoli-della-statistica_08.pdf. Accessed 19 June 2023

Hacker P (2018) Teaching fairness to artificial intelligence: existing and novel strategies against algorithmic discrimination under EU law. Common Market Law Rev 55:1143–1186

Hao L, Chundong W, Yongjie S (2023) Survey on personality recognition based on social media data. J Front Comput Sci Technol 17:1002–1016

Israel G (2015) La matematica e la realtà. Capire il mondo con i numeri. Carocci, Rome

Koen L, Shepherd T (2017) Datafication & discrimination. In: Schäfer MT, van Es K (eds) The datafied society: studying culture through data. Amsterdam University Press, Amsterdam, pp 211–231

Koldinská K (2011) Case law of the European Court of Justice on sex discrimination 2006–2011. Common Market Law Rev 48:1599–1638

Kyaw KS, Tepsongkroh P, Thongkamkaew C, Sasha F (2023) Business intelligent framework using sentiment analysis for smart digital marketing in the E-commerce era. Asia Soc 16:1–23

Li Z (2022) Affinity-based algorithmic pricing: a dilemma for EU data protection law. Comput Law Secur Rev. https://doi.org/10.2139/ssrn.4144571

Lodder AR, Moraiscarvalho J (2022) Online platforms: towards an information tsunami with new requirements on moderation, ranking, and traceability. Eur Bus Law Rev 4:537–556

Longo A, Scorza G (2020) Intelligenza artificiale. L'impatto sulle nostre vite, diritti e libertà. Mondadori, Milan

Lynskey O, Micklitz HW, Rott P (2021), Personalised pricing and personalised commercial practices. In: Helberger N, Lynskey O, Micklitz HW, Rott P, Sax M, Strycharz J (eds) EU consumer protection 2.0. Structural asymmetries in digital consumer markets, a joint report from research conducted under the EUCP2.0 project. BEUC (The European Consumer Organisation), Brussels, pp 92–146

Macchiavelli N (2021) Gender violence and the use of algorithms as an effective tool for the protection of fundamental rights. In: Esteban Dela Rosa F, Gil Ruiz JM, Hinojosa Martínez LM,

Orti Vallejo A, Sánchez Lorenzo SA, Vals Prieto J (eds) Justice, trade, security, and individual freedoms in the digital society. Thomson Reuters Aranzadi, Pamplona, pp 381–398
Maggiolino M (2022) Antitrust, pricing algorithms and the liable humans behind them. J Eur Int IP Law 71:1121–1122
Martínez N, Vinas A, Matute H (2021) Examining potential gender bias in automated-job alerts in the Spanish market. PLoS ONE 16:1–5
Mattarella G (2020) Big Data e accesso al credito degli immigrati: discriminazioni algoritmiche e tutela del consumatore. Giurisprudenza Commerciale 4:696–716
Montinaro R (2022) I sistemi di raccomandazione nelle interazioni tra professionisti e consumatori: il punto di vista del diritto dei consumi. Persona e Mercato 3:368–391
Muir E (2013) The transformative function of EU equality law. Eur Rev Private Law 21:1231–1253
Noble SU (2018) Algorithms of oppression: how search engines reinforce racism. New York University Press, New York
Pardolesi R, Davola A (2019) «Smart contract»: lusinghe ed equivoci dell'innovazione purchessia In: Capriglione F (ed), Liber amicorum Guido Alpa. Wolters Kluwer, Padua, pp 297–314
Peers S, Hervey T, Kenner J, Ward A (eds) (2021) The EU charter of fundamental rights: a commentary. Bloomsbury, Oxford
Perlingieri P (1990) L'informazione come bene giuridico. Rassegna di diritto civile 2:329–358
Pezzoli A, Tonazzi A (2019) Discriminazione e collusione tacita tra lessico, intelligenza artificiale e algoritmi. Analisi giuridica dell'economia 1:201–212
Pisani G (2023) Piattaforme digitali e autodeterminazione. Relazioni sociali, lavoro e diritti al tempo della "governamentalità algoritmica". Mucchi, Modena
Porat A, Strahilevitz JL (2021) Personalizing default rules and disclosure with big data. In: Busch C, De Franceschi A (eds) Algorithmic regulation and personalized law. Beck/Hart, München - Oxford - Baden-Baden, pp 5–51
Porrini D (2000) Asimmetrie informative e concorrenzialità nel mercato assicurativo: che cosa cambia con i "big data"? Mercato concorrenza regole 3:491–514
Porrini D (2016) Risk classification in natural catastrophe insurance: the case of Italy. Int J Financial Res 7:39–49
Resta G (2019) Governare l'innovazione tecnologica: decisioni algoritmiche, diritti digitali e principio di uguaglianza. Politica del diritto 50:199–236
Rodotà S (1997) Tecnopolitica. La democrazia e le nuove tecnologie della comunicazione. Laterza, Rome–Bari
Schmidt N, Stephens BE (2019) An Introduction to artificial intelligence and solutions to the problems of algorithmic discrimination. ArXiv 73:130–144
Shah H (2018) Algorithmic accountability. Philos Trans Roy Soc a: Math Phys Eng Sci 376:1–6. https://doi.org/10.1098/rsta.2017.0362.Accessed30June2023
Simoncini A (2019) L'algoritmo incostituzionale: intelligenza artificiale e il futuro delle libertà. Biodiritto–BioLaw J 1:63–89
Simoncini A, Suweis S (2019) Il cambio di paradigma nell'intelligenza artificiale e il suo impatto sul diritto costituzionale. Rivista internazionale di filosofia del diritto 8:87–106
Smuha N (2019) The EU approach to ethics guidelines for trustworthy artificial intelligence. Comput Law Rev Int 20:97–106
Stark B, Stegmann D, Jürgens P, Magin M (2020) Are algorithms a threat to democracy? The rise of intermediaries: a challenge for public discourse. https://algorithmwatch.org. Accessed 30 June 2023
Timmis S, Broadfoot P, Sutherland R, Oldfield A (2015) Rethinking assessment in a digital age: opportunities, challenges and risks. Br Edu Res J 42:454–476
Tolan S, Miron M, Gomez E, Castillo C (2019) Why machine learning may lead to unfairness: evidence from risk assessment for Juvenile Justice in Catalonia. In: Proceedings of the seventeenth international conference on artificial intelligence and law, pp 83–92. https://doi.org/10.1145/3322640.3326705

Tommasi S (2021) Algoritmi e nuove forme di discriminazione: Uno sguardo al diritto europeo. Revista de Direito Brasileira 26:112–129

Tripathi D, Edla DR, Bablani A, Shukla AK, Reddy B (2021) Experimental analysis of machine learning methods for credit score classification. Prog Artif Intell 10:2–3

Wachter S (2020) Affinity profiling and discrimination by association in online behavioural advertising. Berkeley Technol Law J 35:1–74

Wilson KG (1988) Technologies of control. The new interactive media for the home. University of Wisconsin Press, Chicago

Wójcik MA (2022) Algorithmic discrimination in health care: an EU law perspective. Health Human Rights J 24:93–103

Xenidis R (2018) Multiple discrimination in EU anti-discrimination law: towards redressing complex inequality? In: Belavusau U, Henrard K (eds) EU anti-discrimination law beyond gender. Hart Publishing, Oxford, pp 41–74

Zuddas P (2020) Intelligenza artificiale e discriminazioni. Consulta Online 2:408–425

Zuiderveen Borgesius FJ (2018) Discrimination, artificial intelligence, and algorithmic decision-making. https://rm.coe.int/discrimination-artificial-intelligence-and-algorithmic-decision-making/1680925d73. Accessed 20 June 2023

Zuiderveen Borgesius FJ (2019) Price discrimination, algorithmic decision-making, and European non-discrimination law. Eur Bus Law Rev 31:401–422

Zuiderveen Borgesius FJ (2020) Strengthening legal protection against discrimination by algorithms and artificial intelligence. Int J Human Rights 24:1–22

Chapter 4
Discrimination in the Digital Market: Protection from Different Sides

Abstract This chapter shows that the use of algorithms by digital service providers leads to insidious new forms of discrimination that cannot be protected by European anti-discrimination legislation alone. This legislation has limitations that can be traced back to two factors. Firstly, the European legislation is too closely linked to lists and typical causes of discrimination. Secondly, the European legislation shows gaps regarding indirect discrimination, as it does not provide adequate protection against proxies and hidden discrimination. It is more difficult to identify discrimination in the case of characteristics that are formally neutral, but which recur frequently in protected categories. Considering the scenario described, effective protection of online discrimination cannot be entrusted to sector-specific rules, but to a systematic interpretation, which is inevitably also attentive to the rules on unfair commercial practices and data protection.

Keywords European anti-discrimination legislation · Indirect discrimination · Proxies · GDPR · Unfair commercial practices

4.1 Limits of European Anti-discrimination Law

The use of algorithms by digital service intermediaries leads to insidious new forms of discrimination that cannot be protected solely by European anti-discrimination legislation.[1] In fact, this legislation has limitations that can be traced back to two factors. The European legislation is in fact too closely linked to lists and typical causes

[1] Empirical evidence of bias in automated decision-making will require us to revisit many of the fundamental challenges to the conceptual apparatus of discrimination law—from academic debates about the discipline's normative foundations to courts' reluctance to approach causation through a 'legalistic' lens in the equality context. In these terms Adams-Prassl et al. (2023) p. 145. For an overview of European anti-discrimination legislation, see Wójcik (2022), p. 95. The author points out that "according to article 2 of the Treaty on the European Union, equality is one of the founding values of the EU. Pursuant to article 3 of the treaty, equality, non-discrimination, and social justice also remain the EU's objectives. Furthermore, in Mangold, the European Court of Justice confirmed that non-discrimination constitutes a general principle of EU law". On the fact

S. Tommasi, *The Risk of Discrimination in the Digital Market*,
SpringerBriefs in Law, https://doi.org/10.1007/978-3-031-43640-6_4

of discrimination, so much so that there has long been talk of a general directive on non-discrimination, which has never been had.[2]

The European legislation shows gaps regarding indirect discrimination, as it does not provide adequate protection against proxies and the hidden discrimination they cause,[3] to the extent that it has been pointed out that‹‹the notion of indirect discrimination might become a conceptual 'refuge' to capture the discriminatory wrongs of algorithms››.[4]

Direct discrimination, in fact, immediately identifies the protected category and is, probably, the most easily avoided, for example, by providing, already at the processing and implementation stage, that the algorithms do not base decisions on discriminating elements.[5]

It is more difficult to identify discrimination in the case of characteristics that are formally neutral, but which recur frequently in protected categories.[6]

Just think that a dataset that does not contain explicit data about people's sexual orientation can still give information about people's sexual orientation. The study demonstrates a method for accurately predicting the sexual orientation of Facebook users by analysing friendship associations. The percentage of a given user's friends who self–identify as gay male is strongly correlated with the sexual orientation of that user.[7]

---

that the existing categories of EU anti-discrimination law do not provide an easy fit for algorithmic decision making, see Hacker (2018), p. 1143; Wachter et al. (2021), p. 11.

[2] Gerards and Xenidis (2021), p. 11, in their report, they state that ‹‹at the legal level, such measures notably include adopting the draft Horizontal Directive under negotiation at the Council since 2008 to equalise the scope of EU non-discrimination law, addressing the gaps linked to the exceptions in the material scope of the Gender Goods and Services Directive in relation to the media, advertising and education, and bringing clarity on the prohibition of intersectional discrimination. Turning to the role of the Court of Justice, an expansive interpretation of the personal scope of EU equality law—both in terms of the scope of single protected grounds and the exhaustive nature of the list established in Article 19 TFEU considering the open-ended provision in Article 21 of the Charter—would enhance the law's capacity to address algorithmic discrimination››.

[3] As to the debate on whether a discriminatory intent is necessary to apply the anti-discriminatory legislation see Mattarella (2020), p. 696. With reference to the thesis that discriminatory intent may be lacking, see Morozzo Della Rocca (2002), p. 123; Morozzo Della Rocca (2007), p. 289; Sitzia (2011), p. 99. From a different perspective see Maffeis (2015), p. 171; Navarretta (2020) p. 25. Concerning proxies, there are no unambiguous indications from the Court of Justice of the European Union. See on this point Case C-177/88, Elisabeth Johanna Pacifica Dekker mv. Stichting Vormingscentrum voor Jong Volwassenen (VJV-Centrum) Plus and Case C-668/15, Jyske Finans A/S v Ligebehandlingsnævnet, acting on behalf of Ismar Huskic. In the latter case, the Court of Justice of the European Union ruled that unequal treatment based on the plaintiff's country of origin does not constitute discrimination based on ethnic origin, while in the Dekker case it held that discrimination based on pregnancy is a form of sex discrimination.

[4] Gerards and Xenidis (2021), p. 8.

[5] See Zuiderveen Borgesius (2019), p. 10; Friedman and Nissenbaum (1996); Timmis et al. (2015), p. 1, emphasise that the risk of social exclusion needs to be part of the agenda for any implementation of technology enhanced assessment.

[6] Compare Zuiderveen Borgesius (2023), p. 11.

[7] Zuiderveen Borgesius (2019), p. 13. The author shows that if a bank uses an artificial intelligence system to predict which loan applicants will have problems repaying it, and the artificial intelligence

Another example may be the tax code, which at first glance may appear to be a neutral criterion, to predict defaulting on loans. But suppose that the postcode correlates with racial origin. In that case, if the bank acted based on this prediction and denied loans to the people in that postcode, the practice would harm people from a certain racial origin.

With the multiplication of proxies, moreover, even when eliminating the closest ones, it is difficult to trace back to the most distant ones,[8] so much so that it has been shown that the discriminatory effects of algorithms, however, are most often based on mechanisms that are less visible than the inclusion of a clearly identifiable prohibited criterion in the algorithm. These are often outputs based on past discriminatory decisions.[9]

Under European law, indirect discrimination exists when an apparently neutral criterion or practice is likely to put a person at a disadvantage, not objectively justified by a legitimate aim, and if the means used to achieve that aim are appropriate and necessary (proportionality test).[10]

If we take the example of price discrimination, it cannot be ruled out that abstractly all three exemptions can occur. The objective justification of a legitimate aim has its basis in the freedom to conduct a business under Article 16 of the Charter of Fundamental Rights of the European Union and not in the discriminatory aim. In a situation of competition and not monopoly, if the consumer can procure goods without difficulty at a different price elsewhere, he could be said not to suffer a disproportionate disadvantage.

Discriminatory phenomena achieved through price differentiation may, therefore, remain concealed and unprotected by existing legislation. These are more insidious forms of discrimination that are part of a "strategy of profit maximisation or, in general, of the efficient allocation of resources" and are often concealed by private autonomy and the freedom to choose one's own contractor.[11]

Considering the scenario described, effective protection of online discrimination cannot be entrusted to sector-specific rules, but to a systematic interpretation, which is inevitably also attentive to the rules on unfair commercial practices, data protection and artificial intelligence.[12]

---

system is trained on data that does not contain information on protected characteristics such as skin colour, this does not exclude that the training data cannot be equally discriminatory.

[8] Prince and Schwarcz (2020). The author states that the proxy discrimination is a particularly pernicious subset of disparate impact. Like all forms of disparate impact, it involves a facially neutral practice that disproportionately harms members of a protected class.

[9] See the Report of the Defender of Rights in partnership with the CNIL, Algorithms preventing automated discrimination. https://www.defenseurdesdroits.fr., p. 4.

[10] See Schönberger (2019), p. 184. The author points out that, especially in the health sector, where indirect discrimination is also very common, it is not difficult to pass the propoporality test.

[11] Femia (1996), p. 456. Picker (2003), p. 701, believes that liberal social and economic systems are congenitally discriminatory.

[12] See Zuiderveen Borgesius (2020), p. 3. Compare Perlingieri (2020b) p. 451. Hacker (2018), p. 1143, says that empirical evidence is mounting that artificial intelligence applications threaten to discriminate against legally protected groups. Whereas this evidence, the author shows how

4.2 Data Sharing and Discrimination

At this point, a first fact to be emphasised is that personal data protection rules cannot be disregarded even for the protection against the discriminatory effects of algorithmic determination. The concentration of most of a person's interests in the digital space entails a kind of "compulsory sociability" linked to the inevitability of the circumstance that something about oneself must constantly be shared with others. The inevitable repercussion is that the traditional right to privacy must coexist today, compared to before the digitisation of our daily lives, with the fact that some information must necessarily be communicated to those with whom one comes into contact and to the system that enables it. The alternative is isolation, which concretely can only be imagined in the abstract, since nowadays all our main communications are conveyed by a third party, and in this intermediation, it is not the person in his complexity that comes into play, but his digital identity. In this intermediation carried out by an algorithm, often combined with a physical support, e.g., a smartphone, the system necessarily comes into possession of certain information of the person, otherwise it would be impossible to accept him or her as a user: the technological instrument requires, to be able to dialogue, to exchange data thus sharing them.[13]

In this regard, data protection is an important component of the person-centred approach[14] to technology and the compass in the context of the dual ecological and digital transition of European Union policies.[15]

Data are the food for artificial intelligence systems and, therefore, data regulation is, in essence, the prerequisite regulation for artificial intelligence.[16] Algorithms are based on the direct or indirect collection and algorithmic processing of personal, behavioural data that can reveal certain aspects of people's lives.[17]

---

the concepts of anti-discrimination law may be combined with algorithmic audits and data protection impact assessments to unlock the algorithmic black box. On the need for multi-level anti-discrimination protection, see Capuzzo (2020), p. 89.

[13] See Franzoni (2021), p. 6; Messina (2022), p. 196: Calzolaio (2017), p. 598.

[14] Gilman (2020), p. 1 shows that algorithms analyze data, sort people into categories, and serve as gatekeepers to life's necessities. Yet people remain largely in the dark about these systems, creating an informational asymmetry whose harmful consequences fall most harshly on low-income people.

[15] See COM (2020) 264 final, Communication from the Commission to the European Parliament and the Council, Data protection as a pillar of citizens' empowerment and the EU's approach to the digital transition—two years of application of the General Data Protection Regulation. https://eur-lex.europa.eu. Regarding the circumstance that GDPR rules have the advantage of being based on ex ante and not only ex post protection mechanisms, taking a risk-based approach to prevent the misuse of personal data, compare Li (2022) p. 4; Contissa et al. (2018); Mantelero (2018), p. 299.

[16] Hoeren and Niehoff (2022); De Franceschi and Schulze (2019), p. 22. The author emphasises that European Union started bringing consumer protection in line with the digital age by acknowledging data as counter-performance for the purposes of the new Digital Content Directive. See also Mendola (2023), p. 423; Schmidt-Kessel (2023), p. 153; Gardiner (2022).

[17] About data as fragments of people's lives to which they refer see Tomassini (2020). These are fragments that have a value not because of the intent of the person who left them, often unconsciously, but because they are collected and processed according to a certain procedure by a machine learning algorithm. The value of this data is determined because of the work of the person who collects and

Discriminatory possibilities emerge in particular from profiling and automated data processing systems that develop profiles and are used to make decisions concerning individuals.

It is not surprising, therefore, that a first form of protection can be found in Article 15 of the GDPR.[18] This rule states, in fact, that the data subject shall have the right to obtain from the controller confirmation as to whether or not personal data concerning him or her are being processed, and, where that is the case, access to the personal data and various information, of which the existence of automated decision-making, including profiling, referred to in Article 22(1) and (4) of the GDPR and, at least in these cases, meaningful information about the logic involved, as well as the significance and the envisaged consequences of such processing for the data subject.

Article 22 of the GDPR concerns automated individual decision–making, including profiling, and may also play an important role in protecting people against discrimination.[19] This provision provides that the data subject shall have the right not to be subject to a decision based solely on automated processing, including profiling, which produces legal effects concerning him or her or similarly significantly affects him or her.[20]

The rule is not exempt from criticism. In particular, it was pointed out that Article 22 GDPR offers less protection than Article 9 of Data Protection Convention 108,[21] which does not limit, to a decision based solely on automated processing, the right

---

processes it and by doing so obtains a certain useful result that can be spent on the network. See Franzoni (2021), p. 6.

[18] https://eur-lex.europa.eu. Regarding profiling, reference must be made to Article 4 of the GDPR, which states that profiling means any form of automated processing of personal data consisting of the use of personal data to evaluate certain personal aspects relating to a natural person, in particular to analyse or predict aspects concerning that natural person's performance at work, economic situation, health, personal preferences, interests, reliability, behaviour, location or movements. With reference to the relationship between profiling and technological evolution, compare: Perlingieri (2020a), p. 177; Perlingieri (2018), p. 481; Garofalo (2021), p. 1505; Pellecchia (2018), p. 1209; D' Ippolito (2021), p. 87.

[19] See Mendoza and Bygrave (2017) p. 77, where, in particular, a critical analysis is made of Article 22 of the GDPR in comparison with Article 15 of Directive 95/46/EC of the European Parliament and of the Council of 24 October 1995 on the protection of individuals with regard to the processing of personal data and on the free movement of such data. Article 22 of the GDPR, according to the authors, while offering individuals stronger protection than Article 15 of the 1995 directive, is doubtful to have a significant practical impact on automated profiling.

[20] The prohibition of decisions based solely on automated processing is not absolute, there are exceptions, specified in paragraph 2 of Article 22, namely where such a decision: is necessary for entering into, or performance of, a contract between the data subject and a data controller; is authorised by Union or Member State law to which the controller is subject and which also lays down suitable measures to safeguard the data subject's rights and freedoms and legitimate interests; or is based on the data subject's explicit consent. Compare Grasso (2023) p. 29.

[21] Convention 108, Convention for the protection of individuals regarding the processing of personal data. Council of Europe. https://www.europarl.europa.eu. Convention 108 constitutes the first binding international instrument which is aimed at protecting individuals against abuses which may accompany the collection and processing of personal data, and which seeks to regulate, at the same time, the cross-border flow of personal data.

to obtain, on request, knowledge of the reasoning underlying data processing where the results of such processing are applied to him or her.[22]

What has been said is of relevance with reference to the protection from non-discrimination in that the risks of discrimination are similar, both for fully automated decisions and for those that are only partially automated, and this is due to the so-called "automation bias" or the human tendency to be influenced by the "algorithmically prepared" decision.[23]

Article 22 of the GDPR, moreover, does not cover cases of so–called "microtargeting" and discriminatory advertising solicitation, as happens, for example, when advertising legal aid services in criminal matters is sent only to persons with surnames that reveal the person's African American origin or advertising pharmaceutical products to sick or particularly vulnerable subjects.[24]

Discriminatory targeting can facilitate so-called "predatory inclusion", deliberately targeting poor or vulnerable people with exploitative products like gambling and payday loans.[25]

Numerous studies have shown how "microtargeting" can reinforce stereotypes and discrimination in the labour market.[26]

Discriminatory targeting can facilitate so-called "predatory inclusion", deliberately targeting poor or vulnerable people with exploitative products like gambling and payday loans.[27]

A distinction must be made between the different hypotheses falling within the scope of Article 22 of the GDPR. The following considerations show this.

The data subject, first of all, shall have the right not to be subject to a decision based solely on automated processing, including profiling, which produces legal effects concerning him or her or similarly significantly affects him or her. For this right to be effective, it is a prerequisite that the person, as provided for in Article 15 of the GDPR, is informed of the existence of automated decision–making, including profiling, and, at least in those cases, meaningful information about the logic involved,

---

[22] See Veale and Edwards (2018), p. 398; Pizzetti (2018).

[23] Skitka et al. (1999), p. 991. The authors are referred to for an analysis of some computerised human decision support and aid systems in some common contexts, in comparison with unsupported decisions.

[24] Zadeh et al. (2017).

[25] Griffin (2022), p. 1; MCMillan Cottom (2020), p. 444.

[26] A recent empirical study showed how the targeting of online ads can reinforce stereotyping and segregation on the labour market: during the experiment, researchers used the Facebook advertising platform to neutrally disseminate various employment ads. In the end, cashier positions in supermarkets reached an audience composed of 85% women, while ads for taxi driver positions reached a 75% black audience and ads for lumberjack positions reached an audience that was 90% male and 72% white. A global consensus has emerged among both researchers and policymakers that risks of algorithmic discrimination are pervasive and multifaceted. In this context, understanding these risks and the types of legal challenges they create is key to ensuring equality and combating discrimination. On this point, please refer to Gerards and Xenidis (2021), p. 7; De Franceschi (2022), p. 73; Frosini (2020), p. 402.

[27] Griffin (2022), p. 1.

as well as the significance and the envisaged consequences of such processing for the data subject.

Automated individual decision-making cannot be, therefore, at least in cases falling within the scope of Article 22(1) of the GDPR, a shield for not accounting for the logic used. The fact is important in our perspective because the right to meaningful information about the logic involved by the algorithm may help to identify the possibly discriminatory scope of the activity performed. Also important is the second paragraph of Article 22 of the GDPR, concerning the cases in which decisions based solely on automated processing are permitted. In the cases, the data controller shall implement suitable measures to safeguard the data subject's rights and freedoms and legitimate interests, at least the right to obtain human intervention on the part of the controller, to express his or her point of view and to contest the decision.[28]

These rights of the data subject may include the right not to be discriminated against.

The GDPR in Article 22 bends the logic of algorithms to that of the protection of rights, not allowing them to be used if they cannot be explained and, in some of the cases examined, do not allow for human intervention. Insofar as this is provided for, it allows the rules referred to also be used to protect against discrimination.

On this point, the Italian Supreme Court of Cassation no. 14381 of 2021[29] may be of interest. It states that the requirement of awareness of the consent to the processing of personal data, in the case of a web platform prearranged for the processing of reputational profiles of individuals or legal entities, cannot be considered fulfilled where the algorithm's executive scheme and the elements of which it is composed remain unknown and not knowable by the interested parties.

Interesting, too, is a reading that takes into account that if the right, of the data subject, to obtain from the controller meaningful information about the logic involved, is recognised in the cases provided for in Article 22(1) of the GDPR, a fortiori it must be recognised in the cases provided for in Article 22(2) GDPR, i.e. when the right not to be subject to a decision based solely on automated processing is not provided for.

Even more explicit in recognising a right to non-discriminatory automatized processing in the case of a decision based solely on automated processing is the lesser known but equally important Directive (EU) 2016/680 of the European Parliament and of the Council of 27 April 2016 on the protection of natural persons with regard to the processing of personal data by competent authorities for the purposes of the prevention, investigation, detection or prosecution of criminal offences or the execution of criminal penalties, and on the free movement of such data.[30] The Directive (EU) 2016/680 emphasises the importance of protection of the individual

[28] The regulation appears to convey a clear message: to restore centrality to the human factor, although without the necessary logical and legal precedence of the human agent being an obstacle to technological innovation and to the improvement of the processes that public and private parties put in place. This is what has been affirmed by Pajno et al. (2019), p. 13.

[29] www.italgiure.giustizia.it.

[30] https://eur-lex.europa.eu.

that does not depend on the techniques used, but is equal in cases of automated or manual processing of personal data. It is reiterated, as in the GDPR, that Member States shall provide for a decision based solely on automated processing, including profiling, which produces an adverse legal effect concerning the data subject or significantly affects him or her, to be prohibited unless authorised by Union or Member State law to which the controller is subject and which provides appropriate safeguards for the rights and freedoms of the data subject, at least the right to obtain human intervention on the part of the controller. This is what is stated in Article 11 of the Directive (EU) 2016/680, which prohibits profiling that results in discrimination against natural persons on the basis of personal data revealing racial or ethnic origin, political opinions, religious or philosophical beliefs, or trade union membership, and the processing of genetic data, biometric data for the purpose of uniquely identifying a natural person, data concerning health or data concerning the sex life or sexual orientation of a natural person. Processing of special categories of personal data is only authorised under the strict conditions of Article 10 of the Directive (EU) 2016/680.[31] Notwithstanding the specific regulation of a decision based solely on automated processing in Article 11 of the Directive (EU) 2016/680, this Directive also applies, with specific guarantees, to the processing of personal data wholly or partly by automated means, and to the processing other than by automated means of personal data which form part of a filing system or are intended to form part of a filing system.

The rights of the data subject may not be restricted except in a manner consistent with the Charter of Fundamental Rights of the European Union, and thus, also with Article 21 of the Charter, although specific reference to that Article is only found in whereas 38 of the Directive (EU) 2016/680, specifically referring to processing based solely on automated processing.

On the relationship between automated data processing and non–discrimination is of interest the "Lei Geral de Proteção de Dados Pessoais", law of Brasil 13.709/2018[32] and especially Article 6 of the same law. This article states in point IX, that that personal data processing activities must respect good faith and the principle of non–discrimination, which consists in the impossibility of processing for unlawful or abusively discriminatory purposes. The "Lei Geral de Proteção de Dados Pessoais" is of particular interest also because it is explicit in the sense of the indispensability of the transparency of the algorithm, also for the purpose of assessing its possible discriminatory scope. See, for instance, Article 20 of the "Lei Geral de Proteção de Dados Pessoais", which states that the controller must provide clear and adequate

[31] The Article 10 of the Directive (EU) 2016/680 states that processing of personal data revealing racial or ethnic origin, political opinions, religious or philosophical beliefs, or trade union membership, and the processing of genetic data, biometric data for the purpose of uniquely identifying a natural person, data concerning health or data concerning a natural person's sex life or sexual orientation shall be allowed only where strictly necessary, subject to appropriate safeguards for the rights and freedoms of the data subject, and only: where authorised by Union or Member State law; to protect the vital interests of the data subject or of another natural person; or where such processing relates to data which are manifestly made public by the data subject.

[32] https://brasil.mylex.net/legislacao.

information on the criteria and procedures used for the automated decision and that the national authority may carry out an audit to verify discriminatory aspects in the automated processing of personal data.[33]

Information on the logic used by the algorithm can be a form of protection against potential risks inherent in decision–making processes.[34]

4.3 Non-discrimination and Objective of Maximising the Value of Data in the Economy

The right to the protection of personal data in the GDPR must be balanced with other fundamental rights, including, as we read in whereas 4, the freedom to conduct a business. In fact, whereas 4 of the GDPR states that the processing of personal data should be designed to serve mankind. The right to the protection of personal data must be considered in relation to its function in society and be balanced against other fundamental rights, in accordance with the principle of proportionality.

The provisions of the GDPR emphasise that the right to the protection of personal data, considered in the light of its social function,[35] is explicitly recognised as instrumental to the fulfilment also of economic interests, coessential to the development of the single market.[36]

The information intersects, feeds on itself, and grows to become sophisticated information products, very valuable to the market.[37] The concentration of most of a person's interests in the digital space is also, and above all, considered one of the most important drivers of economic growth.[38]

---

[33] Freire de Carvalho (2020), p. 6.

[34] See Ricciuto (2019), p. 54; Ricciuto (2022); Carapezza Figlia (2022), p. 1372; Tullio (2023), p. 78.

[35] Irti (2021), p. 40, points out that while Article 1 of Directive 95/46/EC stated that Member States shall protect the fundamental rights and freedoms of natural persons, and in particular their right to privacy with respect to the processing of personal data, Article 1(2) of the GDPR, stated that GDPR protects fundamental rights and freedoms of natural persons and in particular their right to the protection of personal data. The author dwells, in particular, on the implications of the different content of the rules in question.

[36] Compare Gentili (2022) p. 707.

[37] Perlingieri (2018), p. 481. The author emphasises that the innovation marks the transition from a conception based exclusively on informed consent to one characterised predominantly by control. The author also states that it is no longer possible to disguise the fact that consent is not sufficient and in fact in some respects misleading and unsuitable to guarantee respect for the person. Compare Francesca (2022), p. 563; Thobani (2015), p. 459; Mignone (2014), p. 14.

[38] Irti (2021), p. 42; Petit and Van Cleynenbreugel (2020), p. 4, underline that Digital businesses and online platforms defy traditional notions of market power grounded in a well-defined relevant product/price. In the context of digital businesses consumers rather pay with their own data or with their time, which may require different tools to analyze market dominance. Often considered as powerful economic actors, a platform is dependent on the ability of the technology underlying it to

The objective of maximising the value of data in the economy and society is also stated by the European Union[39] in the COM (2022) 68 final of 23 February 2022, Proposal for a Regulation of the European Parliament and of the Council on harmonised rules on fair access to and use of data, known as Data Act[40] and in the Regulation (EU) 2022/868 of the European Parliament and of the Council, of 30 May 2022 on European data governance, known as Data Governance Act, which focuses on reliable mechanisms for data sharing and also in order to safeguard fair competition and non–discrimination in relation to the use of data.[41]

It must be emphasised, however, that even if one wishes to waive the confidentiality of one's own data, this does not imply an—among other things impossible and inconceivable—renunciation of one's dignity[42] or the right not to be discriminated against, especially since this right is not identified with a right to equal treatment, but with the right to respect for the Human dignity.[43]

The link between the right not to be discriminated against and respect for human dignity is highlighted also in the Principles, Definitions and Model Rules of European Private Law Draft Common Frame of Reference (DCFR),[44] where it is stated that ‹‹while in general persons should remain free to contract or to refuse to contract with anyone else, this freedom may need to be qualified where it might result in

---

maintain and attract users to its services. The compilation and use of an ever-increasing amount of personal data and big data plays an essential role in this regard.

[39] See Leistner (2021), p. 515; Jabłonowska (2022), p. 67, says that the European Union institutions have recently intensified their efforts to pass new legislation for the digital economy.

[40] The Data Act lays down harmonised rules on making data generated by the use of a product or related service available to the user of that product or service, on the making data available by data holders to data recipients, and on the making data available by data holders to public sector bodies or Union institutions, agencies or bodies, where there is an exceptional need, for the performance of a task carried out in the public interest. In the Data Act, attention is also paid to the fact that the clauses on the provision of data are non-discriminatory. Whereas 41 in fact provides that to compensate for the lack of information on the conditions of different contracts, which makes it difficult for the data recipient to assess if the terms for making the data available are non-discriminatory, it should be on the data holder to demonstrate that a contractual term is not discriminatory. It is not unlawful discrimination, where a data holder uses different contractual terms for making data available or different compensation if those differences are justified by objective reasons. On this point see Orlando (2022a, b); Sganga (2022), p. 65; Caloprisco (2021), p. 169.

[41] See in particular Article 26(2) of the Data Governance Act. On this point compare Alfonsi (2022) p. 294. About the European Strategy Data, see Arisi (2022) p. 33. For a comparison between the GDPR and the Data Governance Act, see Resta (2022), p. 971. The author, p. 984, argues that Articles 15 of the GDPR do not always work at the operational level, either because the incentives needed to overcome the costs of inertia involved in exercising the right are lacking or because the very possibilities of super vision as to how data can be used are limited. The Data Governance Act, on the other hand, prefigures more or less advanced forms of support to individuals both in the pre-consent phase (Art. 12(1)(m)); and in the phase of exercising the data subject's rights and exercising the relevant remedies (Art. 2(1)(11); Art. 10(1)(b)).

[42] Perlingieri (2018), p. 484; Perlingieri (2018), p. 179.

[43] Gentili (2009), p. 207; Hernu (2020), p. 44.

[44] See Alpa et al. (2009), p. 1417; Schulze (2008), p. 11; De Cristofaro (2009); Tommasi (2011), p. 119.

unacceptable discrimination, for example discrimination on the grounds of gender, race or ethnic origin. Discrimination on those grounds is a particularly anti-social form of denying contractual freedom, and indeed the human dignity, of the other party. EU law and the DCFR therefore prohibit these forms of discrimination and provide appropriate remedies››.[45]

It is not, therefore, the different treatment of one person in relation to another that is discriminatory, but the reasons and the manner of that treatment that can make it discriminatory.[46]

It is also necessary to consider the relevance of non-personal data in the operation of artificial intelligence systems and to place limits on the ability of data to interfere in the decision-making process.[47] Thus, limiting the operation of the purpose for which the data are intended would automatically limit their value in economic terms.[48]

What has been said confirms that effective protection from algorithmic discrimination is possible through a systemic and multilevel approach, which enhances the contribution that can also be made by more generic and transversal regulations such as the one on unfair commercial practices. The regulations on unfair commercial practices are even more valuable insofar as they can compress the spaces that are not covered by the GDPR due to the limits that this regulation has with regard to non-personal data and to decisions that are not fully automated.

---

[45] Principles, Definitions and Model Rules of European Private Law Draft Common Frame of Reference (DCFR), Outline Edition, 2009, p. 65 (7). See Books II and III—2:101 to II—2:105 and III—1:105.

[46] For a detailed reconstruction on the point, see Checchini (2019), p. 4. The problem is usually approached in terms of the prevalence of the principle of equality over the principle of contractual freedom, neglecting that these are principles of equal weight operating in different fields, since equality is pertinent to cases of distributive justice: equality in a community, equality before the law. Contract, however, is a case of retributive justice, to which the principle of freedom pertains. On these aspects compare Galgano (2002), p. 53; Buonocore (2008), p. 551; Gentili (2009), p. 221. The author states that individual relationships do not lend themselves to being subjected to a judgement of equality of treatment which, in fact, presupposes the existence of two terms to be compared and a criterion of comparison that are not found in a strictly individual relationship. For a critique of attempts to transfer aspirations of distributive justice onto the contract, see D'Amico (2019), p. 48. With specific reference to the impact of the principle of non-discrimination in contractual relations, see Piraino (2015) p. 233; Perlingieri (2017), p. 1629, says that each contract is characterised by its own "proclaimed social function", which represents the reference parameter for appreciating its merits. Roppo (2011), p. 79, considers that to the extent that it is the realm of freedom, the contract can also be the realm of inequality and discrimination, based on the free choices of the contracting parties. For the author, private autonomy is intrinsically discriminatory and between contract and equality there is an ambiguous relationship, which suffers from the ambiguity inherent in the very idea of equality: declined, as is well known, in terms of formal equality or substantial equality. See also Roppo (2020), p. 28.

[47] See Resta (2019), p. 211. The author suggests distinguishing issues concerning personal data from those concerning non-personal data. For a comparison between the Artificial Intelligence Act and the EU data protection acquis see Mazzini and Scalzo (2022) p. 35. Regarding the relationship between GDPR and consumer discipline, compare Pagliantini (2022), p. 1560.

[48] Lanni (2020), p. 120.

4.4 Discrimination in the Digital Market and Unfair Commercial Practices Directive

To demonstrate that unfair commercial practices rules can also contribute to protection in a non-discriminatory function, it may be useful to take the example of the personalisation of prices in the digital market.[49] Algorithmic pricing, in fact, creates the risk of loss of decision-making autonomy, influencing or even distorting the economic behaviour of the consumer.[50]

Software with the characteristics of artificial intelligence has the power to influence people's decisions and behaviour to an extent that was unthinkable just a few years ago. It is no coincidence that subsections (a) and (b) of Article 5 of the Artificial Intelligence Act use the terminology "to materially distort", which is identical to the terminology used in the Directive 2005/29/EC of the European Parliament and of the Council of 11 May 2005 concerning unfair business-to-consumer commercial practices in the internal market,[51] known as Unfair Commercial Practices Directive.[52]

It is to be considered contrary to the requirements of professional diligence and likely to materially distort the economic behaviour of the average consumer a practice is based on a bait price that the algorithm has been able to work out on the basis of the consumer's data and behaviour.

Here, too, a form of protection may be provided by transparency rules. On this point, the rules on commercial practices make a significant contribution.[53]

---

[49] Auer (2021), p. 14, fears the danger of moving backwards from the intellectual standards of decades, if not centuries, about discrimination. Montinaro (2022), p. 352, points out that the omnibus directive refers to the GDPR and that from this it can be deduced that the unfairness of the practice is not excluded by mere compliance with the obligation of transparency of parameters. In particular, the author observes that there could be the collection of data to personalise prices without the consent of consumers; the use of data to personalise prices when such data were requested for other stated reasons; the use of knowledge of a specific vulnerable condition obtained through real-time observation of an individual consumer.

[50] See Li (2022), p. 4. On the fact that artificial Intelligence (AI) systems are increasingly being deployed by marketing entities in connection with consumers' interaction and manipulation as a substantive legal measure for drawing the line between fair and unfair practices, see Galli (2022), p. 1. On how instruments in EU consumer law could alleviate certain asymmetries in power and information, see Durovic and Watson (2022), p. 153. In particular, the authors point out that consumer data has become a driving force in the digital economy. As the number of data interactions increases, so too the insights into ever more intimate aspects of one's daily life, behaviour and personality. Amongst the various products and services, one innovative advancement in the world of data-driven technology stands out as deserving particular attention: the capability to infer emotions from (personal) data and to use such information to respond to an individual's needs on a highly intimate level. Whereas the technology has considerable potential, it is controversial not least due to the highly sensitive and private nature of emotions but also due to its questionable reliability as well as potential adverse effects.

[51] https://eur-lex.europa.eu. Compare Capobianco (2018), p. 13.

[52] Orlando (2022a, b), p. 357. Compare Barenghi (2020), p. 195; Barba (2021), p. 104.

[53] Duivenvoorde (2022), p. 43. The authors show that despite the liability exemptions in the E-Commerce Directive and the Digital Services Act, the Unfair Commercial Practices Directive provides significant room to hold on-line marketplaces liable.

According to Directive 2019/2161/EU, known as Omnibus Directive,[54] provides that traders may personalise the price of their offers for specific consumers or specific categories of consumer based on automated decision-making and profiling of consumer behaviour allowing traders to assess the consumer's purchasing power.[55] Consumers should therefore be clearly informed when the price presented to them is personalised on the basis of automated decision-making, so that they can take into account the potential risks in their purchasing decision.[56]

In these respects, is also of interest Article 3 of the Directive 2019/2161/EU where it is stated that amendments to the Directive 2005/29/EC should include that when providing consumers with the possibility to search for products offered by different traders or by consumers on the basis of a query in the form of a keyword, phrase or other input, irrespective of where transactions are ultimately concluded, general information, made available in a specific section of the online interface that is directly and easily accessible from the page where the query results are presented, on the main parameters determining the ranking of products presented to the consumer as a result of the search query and the relative importance of those parameters, as opposed to other parameters, shall be regarded as material.[57]

A person can understand the potential risks of the purchase decision process when they realise that the price has been personalised. In other words, it is one thing to know that a branded bag is being offered to everyone at a certain, particularly high price, and another to know that it is being offered to me at that particularly high price because the algorithm knows that I am a fan of that brand.

It should not be overlooked that algorithmic discrimination also poses specific problems due to the characteristics of algorithms and artificial intelligence systems. The possible incidence of discrimination in the most diverse spheres of people's lives does not obviate the need for a systemic and general approach, which identifies a general frame of reference also for the digital environment.[58]

It is therefore necessary to dwell on a more in–depth analysis of the Artificial Intelligence Act.

---

[54] The Directive (EU) 2019/2161 of the European Parliament and of the Council, of 27 November 2019, amending Council Directive 93/13/EEC and Directives 98/6/EC, 2005/29/EC and 2011/83/EU of the European Parliament and of the Council as regards the better enforcement and modernisation of Union consumer protection rules. https://eur-lex.europa.eu.

[55] See whereas 45.

[56] Benedetti (2021), p. 413, analyses the implications of no longer seeking out potential customers with contractual proposals, but offering them what we already know they will accept, by means of invasive profiling against which there is a need for new forms of protection.

[57] See Guffanti Pesenti (2021), p. 635.

[58] See Smuha et al. (2021), p. 23. The authors criticise Article 5(c) of the Proposed Artificial Intelligence Act by stating that this article focuses on social behaviour or known or predicted personal or personality characteristics, while it is well documented that proxies may be employed for where such personal data is protected. These proxies could be drawn from factors not mentioned in the Article, such geographical location (postcodes, etc.). Scoring on these measures can be as discriminatory and devastating for individuals as those drawn from the characteristics included in the Proposal.

References

Adams-Prassl J, Binns R, Kelly-Lyth A (2023) Directly discriminatory algorithms. Mod Law Rev 86:144–175

Alfonsi R (2022) Approvato il Data Governance Act: Regolamento (Ue) 2022/868 del 30 maggio 2022 sulla governance europea dei dati. Persona e Mercato. Osservatorio OGID 8:294–298

Alpa G, Iudica G, Perfetti U, Zatti P (eds) (2009) Il Draft common frame of reference del diritto privato europeo. Cedam, Padua

Arisi M (2022) Open knowledge. Access and re–use of research data in the European Union open data directive and the implementation in Italy. Ital Law J 8:34–73

Auer M (2021) Granular norms and the concept of law: a critique. In: Busch C, De Franceschi A (eds) Algorithmic regulation and personalized law. CH Beck/Harts, München - Oxford - Baden-Baden, pp 137–151

Barenghi A (2020) Diritto dei consumatori. Wolters Kluwer, Milan

Barba A (2021) Capacità del consumatore e funzionamento del mercato. Valutazione e divieto delle pratiche commerciali. Giappichelli, Turin

Benedetti AM (2021) Contratto, algoritmi e diritto civile transnazionale: cinque questioni e due scenari. Rivista di diritto civile 3:411–423

Buonocore V (2008) Principio di uguaglianza e diritto commerciale. Giurisprudenza commerciale 35:551–582

Caloprisco F (2021) Data Governance Act. Condivisione e "altruismo" dei dati. Quaderni Aisdue 2:169–188

Calzolaio S (2017) Protezione dei dati personali. In: Dig Disc Pubbl Agg. Utet Giuridica—Wolters Kluwer, Turin, pp 594–635

Capobianco E (2018) Le pratiche commerciali scorrette nel settore bancario. Diritto del mercato assicurativo e finanziario 3:13–29

Capuzzo G (2020) "Do algorithms dream about electric sheep?" Percorsi di studio in tema di discriminazione e processi decisori algoritmici tra le due sponde dell'Atlantico. Rivista di diritto dei media 2:89–106

Carapezza Figlia G (2022) "L'equivoco della privacy". Circolazione dei dati personali e tutela della persona. Jus Civile 5:1372–1377

Checchini B (2019) Discriminazione contrattuale e dignità della persona. Giappichelli, Turin

Contissa G, Docter K, Lagioia F, Lippi M, Micklitz HW, Przemysla P, Sartor G, Torroni P (2018) Claudette meets Gdpr: automating the evaluation of privacy policies using artificial intelligence. European Consumer Organisation (BEUC) study report. http://hdl.handle.net/1814/60795. Accessed 10 June 2022

D'Amico G (2019) Giustizia contrattuale e contratti asimmetrici. Europa e diritto privato 1:1–49

De Cristofaro G (ed) (2009) I «Principi» del diritto comunitario dei contratti. Acquis communautaire e diritto privato europeo. Giappichelli, Turin

De Franceschi A (2022) Consumers' vulnerability in the digital economy: personal data as counterperformance and digital obsolescence. Eur J Consum Law 2:73–93

D'Ippolito G (2021) Profilazione e pubblicità targettizzata online. Real–Time Bidding e behavioural advertising. ESI, Naples

Duivenvoorde B (2022) The liability of online marketplaces under the unfair commercial practices directive, the e–commerce directive and the digital services act. J Eur Consum Market Law 11:43–52

Durovic M, Watson J (2022) AI, Consumer data protection and privacy, In: Ienca M, Pollicino O, Liguori L, Stefanini E, Andorno R (eds) The cambridge handbook of information technology, life sciences and human rights. Cambridge University Press, Cambridge, pp 273–287

Femia P (1996) Interessi e conflitti culturali nell'autonomia privata e nella responsabilità civile. ESI, Naples

Francesca M (2022) Il grande gioco. Buon costume e buon costume stipulativo alla prova dei social network. Teoria e prassi del diritto 2:559–572

De Franceschi A, Schulze R (2019) New challenges and perspectives. In: De Franceschi A, Schulze R, Graziadei M, Pollicino O, Riente F, Sica S, Sirena P (eds.), Digital revolution–new challenges for law. Data protection, artificial intelligence, smart products, blockchain technology and virtual currencies, Beck/Hart, München-Baden-Baden, pp 1–15

Franzoni M (2021) Lesione dei diritti della persona, tutela della privacy e intelligenza artificiale. Jus Civile 1:4–21

Freire de Carvalho B (2020) Discriminação algorítmica e transparência na lei geral de proteção de dados pessoais. Revista de Direito e as Novas Tecnologias. https://bd.tjdft.jus.br/jspui/handle/tjdft/49512. Accessed 20 June 2023

Friedman B, Nissenbaum H (1996) Bias in computer systems. ACM Trans Inf Syst 14:330–347

Frosini TE (2020) Le sfide attuali del diritto ai dati personali. In: Perlingieri P, Giova S, Prisco I (eds) Il trattamento algoritmico dei dati tra etica, diritto ed economia. ESI, Naples, pp 395–402

Galgano F (2002) Il negozio giuridico. Giuffrè, Milan

Galli F (2022) Algorithmic marketing and EU law on unfair commercial practices. Springer, Cham

Gardiner C (2022) Unfair contract terms in the digital age. The challenge of protecting European consumers in the online marketplace. Edward Elgar, Cheltenham

Garofalo G (2021) Identità digitale e diritto all'oblio: questioni aperte all'indomani dell'approvazione del GDPR. Diritto di famiglia e delle persone 3:1506–1518

Gentili A (2009) Il principio di non discriminazione nei rapporti civili. Rivista critica del diritto privato 2:207–231

Gentili A (2022) La volontà nel contesto digitale: interessi del mercato e diritti delle persone. Rivista trimestrale di diritto e procedura civile 76:702–716

Gerards J, Xenidis R (2021) Algorithmic discrimination in Europe: challenges and opportunities for gender equality and non discrimination law. European Commission, Directorate-General for Justice and Consumers. Publications Office. https://data.europa.eu/doi/10.2838/544956

Gilman ME (2020) Poverty lawgorithms: a poverty lawyer's guide to fighting automated decision–making harms on low–income communities. Data Soc. https://ssrn.com/abstract=3699650. Accessed 20 June 2023

Grasso AG (2023) GDPR Feasibility and algorithmic non-statutory discrimination. ESI, Naples

Griffin R (2022) Tackling discrimination in targeted advertising: US regulators take very small steps in the right direction—but where is the EU? https://verfassungsblog.de/targete-ad. Accessed 19 July 2023

Guffanti Pesenti L (2021) Pratiche commerciali scorrette e rimedi nuovi. La difficile trasposizione dell'art. 3, co. 1, N. 5), dir. 2019/2161/UE. Europa e diritto privato 4:635–683

Hacker P (2018) Teaching fairness to artificial intelligence: existing and novel strategies against algorithmic discrimination under EU law. Common Mark Law Rev 55:1143–1185

Hernu R (2020) Le principe d'égalité et le principe de non–discrimination dans la jurisprudence de la CJUE. https://www.conseil-constitutionnel.fr. Accessed 19 July 2023

Hoeren T, Niehoff M (2022) Artificial intelligence and data protection law. In: Corrales Compagnucci M, Wilson M, Fenwick M, Forgó N, Bärnighausen T (eds) AI in eHealth: human autonomy. Data Governance and Privacy in Healthcare. Cambridge University Press, Cambridge, pp 147–165

Irti C (2021) Consenso «negoziato» e circolazione dei dati personali. Giappichelli, Turin

Jabłonowska A (2022) Consumer protection in the age of data-driven behaviour modification. J Eur Consum Mark Law 11:67–71

Lanni S (2020) Dataquake: intelligenza artificiale e discriminazione del consumatore. Nuovo diritto civile 2:97–123

Leistner M (2021) The commission's digital markets and services package—new rules for big tech and big data. J Eur Int IP 70:515–516

Li Z (2022) Affinity–based algorithmic pricing: a dilemma for EU data protection law. Comput Law Secur Rev. https://doi.org/10.2139/ssrn.4144571

Maffeis D (2015) Il diritto contrattuale antidiscriminatorio nelle indagini dottrinali recenti. Le nuove leggi civili e commentate 1:161–180

Mantelero A (2018) La gestione del rischio nel GDPR: limiti e sfide nel contesto dei big data e delle applicazioni di Artificial intelligence. In: Mantelero A, Poletti D (eds), Regolare la tecnologia. Il Reg. UE 2016/679 e la protezione dei dati personali. Un dialogo tra Italia e Spagna. University Press, Pisa, pp 289–305
Mattarella G (2020) Big data e accesso al credito degli immigrati: discriminazioni algoritmiche e tutela del consumatore. Giurisprudenza commerciale 4:696–716
Mazzini G, Scalzo S (2022) The proposal for the artificial intelligence act: considerations around some key concepts. In: Camardi C (ed) La via europea per l'intelligenza artificiale. Atti del Convegno del Progetto Dottorale di Alta Formazione in Scienze Giuridiche Ca' Foscari Venezia, 25–26 novembre 2021, Wolters Kluwer–Cedam, Milan pp. 21–51
McMillan Cottom T (2020) Where platform capitalism and racial capitalism meet: the sociology of race and racism in the digital society. Sociology of Race and Ethnicity, 6(4):441–449. https://doi.org/10.1177/2332649220949473
Mendola A (2023) Libertà di espressione e "costo" del consenso nell'era della condivisione digitale. Analisi comparatistica. Wolters Kluwer-Cedam, Milan
Mendoza I, Bygrave LA (2017) The right not to be subject to automated decisions based on profiling. In: Synodinou T, Jougleux P, Markou C, Prastitou T (eds) EU Internet law. Springer, Cham, pp 77–98
Messina D (2022) La proposta di regolamento europeo in materia di Intelligenza Artificiale: verso una "discutibile" tutela individuale di tipo consumer-centric nella società dominata dal "pensiero artificiale." Rivista di diritto dei media 2:196–232
Mignone C (2014) Identità della persona e potere di disposizione, ESI, Naples
Montinaro R (2022) I sistemi di raccomandazione nelle interazioni tra professionisti e consumatori: il punto di vista del diritto dei consumi. Persona e Mercato 3:368–391
Morozzo Della Rocca P (2002) Gli atti discriminatori nel diritto civile, alla luce degli artt. 43 e 44 del T.U. sull'immigrazione. Il diritto di famiglia e delle persone 31:112–147
Morozzo Della Rocca P (2007) Le discriminazioni nei contratti di scambio di beni e servizi. In: Barbera M (eds) Il nuovo diritto antidiscriminatorio. Il quadro nazionale e comunitario. Giuffrè, Milan, pp 289–341
Navarretta E (2020) Principio di eguaglianza e diritto civile. Questione giustizia 1:23–27
Orlando S (2022a) Regole di immissione sul mercato e «pratiche di intelligenza artificiale» vietate nella proposta di Artificial Intelligence Act. Persona e Mercato 3:346–367
Orlando S (2022b) Verso il Data Act: la proposta di Regolamento del Parlamento e del Consiglio su regole armonizzate sull'accesso equo e l'uso dei dati (legge sui dati) COM(2022) 68 final del 23.2.2022. Persona e Mercato. Osservatorio OGID 1:166–168
Pagliantini S (2022) L'attuazione minimalista della Dir. 2019/770/UE: riflessioni sugli artt. 135 octies-135 vicies ter c. cons. La nuova disciplina dei contratti b-to-c per la fornitura di contenuti e servizi digitali. Nuove leggi civili commentate 6:1499–1560
Pajno A, Bassini M, De Gregorio G, Macchia M, Patti FP, Pollicino O, Quattrocolo S, Simeoli D, Sirena P (2019) AI: profili giuridici. Intelligenza Artificiale: criticità emergenti e sfide per il giurista. Rivista di BioDiritto 3:205–235
Pellecchia E (2018) Profilazione e decisioni automatizzate al tempo della black box society: qualità dei dati e leggibilità dell'algoritmo nella cornice della responsible research and innovation. Le nuove leggi civili commentate 5:1209–1236
Perlingieri P (2017) «Controllo» e «conformazione» degli atti di autonomia negoziale. In Caterini E, Di Nella L, Flamini A, Mezzasoma L, Polidori S (eds) Scritti in onore di Vito Rizzo. II. ESI, Naples pp 1635–1657
Perlingieri P (2018) Privacy digitale e protezione dei dati personali tra persona e mercato. Il Foro napoletano 2:481–484
Perlingieri C (2020a) Creazione e circolazione del bene prodotto dal trattamento algoritmico dei dati. In: Perlingieri P, Giova S, Prisco I (eds) Il trattamento algoritmico dei dati tra etica, diritto ed economia, ESI, Naples, pp 177–197

Perlingieri P (2020b) Il diritto civile nella legalità costituzionale. II. Fonti e interpretazione. ESI, Naples
Petit N, Van Cleynenbreugel P (2020) Questionnaire Topic 3: EU Competition Law and the Digital Economy. In: Mândrescu D (ed) EU Competition Law and the Digital Economy: Protecting Free and Fair Competition in an Age of Technological (R)evolution. The XXIX FIDE congress in The Hague. 2020 Congress Publications. Eleven international publishing, Chicago, pp 1–8
Picker E (2003) L'antidiscriminazione come programma per il diritto privato. Rivista critica del diritto privato 21: 687–703
Piraino F (2015) Il diritto europeo e la «giustizia contrattuale». Europa e diritto privato 2:233–293
Pizzetti F (2018) Intelligenza artificiale, protezione dei dati personali e regolazione. Giappichelli, Turin
Prince A, Schwarcz DB (2020) Proxy discrimination in the age of artificial intelligence and big data. Iowa Law Rev 105:1257–1318
Resta G (2019) Governare l'innovazione tecnologica: decisioni algoritmiche, diritti digitali e principio di uguaglianza. Politica del diritto 50:199–236
Resta G (2022) Pubblico, privato e collettivo nel sistema europeo di governo dei dati. Rivista trimestrale di diritto pubblico 4:971–995
Ricciuto V (2019) La patrimonializzazione dei dati personali. Contratto e mercato nella ricostruzione del fenomeno. In: Cuffaro V, D'Orazio R, Ricciuto V (eds) I dati personali nel diritto europeo. Giappichelli, Turin, pp 23–59
Ricciuto V (2022) L'equivoco della privacy. Persona vs dato personale. ESI, Naples
Roppo V (2011) Il contratto. Giuffrè, Milan
Roppo V (2020) Contrastare le disuguaglianze nelle relazioni contrattuali: fra diritto comune dei contratti e diritto dei contratti del mercato. Questione giustizia 1:28–32
Schmidt-Kessel M (2023) La responsabilità contrattuale del gestore di una piattaforma per la protezione dei dati personali del cliente nella prospettiva dei requisiti di qualità dell'adempimento. Pactum 1:153–162
Schönberger D (2019) Artificial intelligence in healthcare: a critical analysis of the legal and ethical implications. Int J Law Inf Technol 27:171–203
Schulze R (2008) Common frame of reference and existing EC contract law. Sellier de Gruyter, Munich
Sganga C (2022) Ventisei anni di Direttiva Database alla prova della nuova Strategia Europea per i Dati: evoluzioni giurisprudenziali e percorsi di riforma. Diritto dell'informazione e dell'informatica 3:657–710
Sitzia L (2011) Pari dignità e discriminazione. ESI, Naples
Skitka J, Mosier KL, Burdick M (1999) Does automation bias decision–making? Int J Hum Comput Stud 5:991–1006
Smuha NA, Ahmed–Rengers E, Harkens A, Li W, MacLaren J, Piselli R, Yeung K (2021) How the EU can achieve legally trustworthy AI: a response to the European commission's proposal for an Artificial Intelligence Act. https://doi.org/10.2139/ssrn.3899991
Thobani S (2015) Il consenso al trattamento dei dati come condizione per la fruizione di servizi online. In: Perlingieri C, Ruggieri L (eds), Internet e Diritto civile. ESI, Naples, pp 459–484
Timmis S, Broadfoot P, Sutherland R, Oldfield A. (2015) Rethinking assessment in a digital age: opportunities, challenges and risks. Br Edu Res J 42:454–476
Tomassini L (2020) Il grande salto: L'uomo, il digitale e la più importante evoluzione della nostra storia. Luiss University Press, Rome
Tommasi S (2011) La non discriminazione nel DCFR. Rivista critica del diritto privato 1:119–128
Tullio J (2023) Riflessioni sulla disposizione dei dati personali nei negozi di adesione a piattaforme online. Tecnologia e diritto 1:78–105
Veale M, Edwards L (2018) Clarity, surprises, and further questions in the article 29 working party draft guidance on automated decision-making and profiling'. Comput Law Secur Rev 34:398–404

Wachter S, Mittelstadt B, Russell C (2021) Why fairness cannot be automated: Bridging the gap. between EU non–discrimination law and AI. Comput Law Secur Rev 41:1–72
Wójcik MA (2022) Algorithmic discrimination: an eu law perspective. Health Hum Rights 24:93–103
Zadeh NK, Robertson K, Green JA (2017) 'At–risk' individuals' responses to direct to consumer advertising of prescription drugs: a nationally representative cross–sectional study. BMJ 7:1–10
Zuiderveen Borgesius FJ (2019) Discrimination, artificial intelligence, and algorithmic decision–making. https://rm.coe.int/discrimination-artificial-intelligence-and-algorithmic-decision-making/1680925d73. Accessed 30 May 2023
Zuiderveen Borgesius FJ (2020) Strengthening legal protection against discrimination by algorithms. Int J Hum Rights 24:1–22
Zuiderveen Borgesius FJ (2023) Digitale discriminatie en differentiatie: het recht is er nog niet klaar voor. https://papers.ssrn.com/sol3/papers.cfm?abstract_id=4520646. Accessed 31 July 2023

Chapter 5
Risk-Based Approach in the Digital Services Act and in the Artificial Intelligence Act

Abstract An important innovation of the Digital Services Act is that it considers the risk of discrimination as a systemic risk. This can be seen from Article 34 of the Digital Services Act, which refers to systemic risks as any actual or foreseeable negative effects for the exercise of fundamental rights (and the right to non-discrimination is specifically mentioned here). A comparison between the Digital Services Act and the Artificial Intelligence Act is necessary because digital service providers are increasingly using artificial intelligence systems, and therefore it is necessary that the rules of the Digital Services Act and those of the Artificial Intelligence Act do not conflict. It would not be consistent for risks that are unacceptable under the Artificial Intelligence Act to be acceptable under the Digital Services Act or qualified as a systemic risk.

Keywords Artificial intelligence act · Systemic risks · Unacceptable risk · Fundamental rights

5.1 Discrimination as a Systemic Risk

An important innovation of the Digital Services Act is that it considers the risk of discrimination as a systemic risk. This can be seen from Article 34 of the Digital Services Act, which refers to systemic risks as any actual or foreseeable negative effects for the exercise of fundamental rights. The right to non-discrimination is specifically mentioned here.

The focus on the risk of discrimination as a systemic risk is an element of protection that the Digital Services Act adds to the protection of the right to non-discrimination on the assumption that the very large online platforms and very large online search engines may cause societal risks, different in scope and impact from those caused by smaller platforms. There is, therefore, a correlation between dimensions of platform and more stringent obligations apply related to the number of reachable recipients, from which the social impact of the related risks is proportionally deduced.

S. Tommasi, *The Risk of Discrimination in the Digital Market*,
SpringerBriefs in Law, https://doi.org/10.1007/978-3-031-43640-6_5

The Digital Services Act counteracts systemic risks by imposing on large online platforms a risk assessment activity that is preparatory to the adoption of reasonable, proportionate and effective mitigation measures tailored to the specific systemic risks identified.[1]

The results of the assessment of these risks and of the relative mitigation measures are the subject of a report that the very large online platforms must transmit to the Digital Services Coordinator and to the Commission, in conformity with the Transparency Reporting Obligations of Article 15 of the Digital Service Act. Therefore, a complex bureaucratic apparatus is set in motion and supports the platforms in managing risks, not without some criticalities. It can be pointed out, for instance, that the Digital Services Act, on the one hand, outlines a detailed regulatory framework, setting itself objectives of harmonisation and certainty of the applicable discipline, and on the other relies excessively on self-regulation and codes of conduct. Article 45 of the Digital Services Act states, in fact, that where significant systemic risks within the meaning of Article 34(1) emerge and concern several very large online platforms or very large online search engines, the Commission «may invite the providers of very large online platforms concerned or the providers of very large online search engines concerned, and other providers of very large online platforms, of very large online search engines, of online platforms and of other intermediary services, as appropriate, as well as relevant competent authorities, civil society organisations and other relevant stakeholders, to participate in the drawing up of codes of conduct, including by setting out commitments to take specific risk mitigation measures, as well as a regular reporting framework on any measures taken and their outcomes». As if to say that with respect to strategic choices concerning systematic risks, everything is back in the hands of the platforms and the regulations that they spontaneously give themselves, despite the articulated regulatory and bureaucratic architecture that the Digital Services Act aims to design.

5.2 Digital Services Act and Artificial Intelligence Act: Harmonized Rules?

The Digital Services Act and the Artificial Intelligence Act are destined to be an indispensable reference point in the regulation of the future, which, precisely because of the rapid and unstoppable technological change, is increasingly unpredictable and different from the past.[2] Both regulatory acts are based on a model focused on risk and its management.[3]

---

[1] See Achleitner (2022), p. 6.

[2] Compare Benedetti (2021), p. 416; Herbosch (2022), p. 14.

[3] Finocchiaro (2022), p. 303. The author points out that this is a model already chosen in the GDPR, with the difference that in the GDPR the management system is based on accountability and risk assessment by the data controller, as the party best placed to manage the risk. In the Proposed

A comparison between the Digital Services Act and the Artificial Intelligence Act is necessary because, as demonstrated in the chapter on algorithmic discrimination, digital service providers are increasingly using artificial intelligence systems, and therefore it is necessary that the rules of the Digital Services Act and those of the Artificial Intelligence Act do not conflict.

The complexities are obvious. The first to be addressed concerns the coordination between the Digital Services Act and the Artificial Intelligence Act.[4]

It would not be consistent for risks that are unacceptable under the Artificial Intelligence Act to be acceptable under the Digital Services Act or qualified as a systemic risk. The latter, in fact, under the Digital Services Act are not prohibited but, rather, considered unavoidable, even if to be mitigated under Article 35 of the Digital Services Act.

It follows that a brokerage service provider may not use artificial intelligence systems that generate unacceptable risks, even in the absence of an express provision in the Digital Services Act.

For example, a digital services intermediary may not, pursuant to Article 5 of the Artificial Intelligence Act, use an artificial intelligence system that deploys subliminal techniques beyond a person's consciousness or purposefully manipulative or deceptive techniques, with the objective to or the effect of materially distorting a person's or a group of persons' behaviour by appreciably impairing the person's ability to make an informed decision, thereby causing the person to take a decision that that person would not have otherwise taken in a manner that causes or is likely to cause that person, another person or group of persons significant harm.[5] Not even can use a artificial intelligence system that exploits any of the vulnerabilities of a person or a specific group of persons, including characteristics of such person's or a such group's known or predicted personality traits or social or economic situation age, physical or mental ability with the objective or to the effect of materially distorting the behaviour of that person or a person pertaining to that group in a manner that causes or is likely to cause that person or another person significant harm.[6] This is a first check to which the use of artificial intelligence systems by digital service intermediaries should be subjected, as they must also conduct their activities in accordance with the Digital Services Act.

Artificial Intelligence Act, the approach is different because it is the legislator who decides which are the high-risk systems and how the risk they pose is to be dealt with.

[4] Orlando (2022), p. 346 highlights a lack of coordination between the Proposal for a Regulation on the transparency and targeting of political advertising, (COM(2021) 731 final) in https://commission.europa.eu and with the Proposal for a Directive on adapting non-contractual civil liability rules to artificial intelligence (Artificial Intelligence Liability Directive), COM (2022) 496 final. https://commission.europa.eu. Compare Tommasi (2023), p. 280.

[5] On the problems associated with the knowledge that future innovations will enhance the possibilities for manipulating thoughts and behaviour, and they threaten to cause serious harm to individuals as well as to society as a whole, see Neuwirth (2023).

[6] See Amendments 215 and 216 of the Amendments adopted by the European Parliament on 14 June 2023 on the proposal for a regulation of the European Parliament and of the Council on laying down harmonized rules on artificial intelligence (Artificial Intelligence Act) and amending certain Union legislative acts (COM(2021)0206 – C9-0146/2021 –2021/0106(COD))1.

Full of interesting developments, also from a practical point of view, is the relationship between systemic risks under the Digital Services Act and high-risk systems as defined by the Artificial Intelligence Act.

Negative effects for the exercise of fundamental rights are classified by the Digital Services Act as systemic risks and, at the same time, the Artificial Intelligence Act contains classification rules for high-risk artificial intelligence systems, in addition to those provided for in Article 6 and Annex 3.

From reading the Artificial Intelligence Act, and in particular Article 7, it can be inferred that high-risk systems are those that pose a risk of harm to the health and safety, or a risk of adverse impact on fundamental rights, to the environment, or to democracy and the rule of law[7]; risk which, in the case of systems not covered by the Annex, must be assessed as equivalent to or greater than that of the artificial intelligence systems referred to in Annex 3.

Thus, systems that adversely affect fundamental rights may, in some cases, be among those considered high-risk by the Artificial Intelligence Act and generate what the Digital Services Act considers to be systemic risks. In both cases, the risk of negative effects on fundamental rights is not considered unacceptable, but merely a risk against which precautions must be taken.[8]

This does not imply that there is a perfect coincidence between systemic risk under the Digital Service Act and high risk under the Artificial Intelligence Act that no coordination problems arise. Suffice it to say that high-risk systems under the Proposed Artificial Intelligence Act are only those intended for use in the areas listed in points 1–8 of Annex 3 of the same proposal, although, according to the Amendment 238 of the Amendments adopted by the European Parliament on 14 June 2023,[9] the Commission will be empowered to adopt delegated acts by adding or modifying areas or use cases of high-risk artificial intelligence systems.

The coordination requirements are not limited to those highlighted.

The Artificial Intelligence Act considers the risk of significant harm to be unacceptable if caused by an artificial intelligence system deploying ‹‹subliminal techniques beyond a person's consciousness or purposefully manipulative or deceptive techniques, with the objective to or the effect of materially distorting a person's or a group of persons' behaviour by appreciably impairing the person's ability to make an informed decision, thereby causing the person to take a decision that that person

[7] Smuha et al. (2021), p. 14. The authors argue that the Proposal fails to reflect fundamental rights as claims with enhanced moral and legal status, which subjects any rights interventions to a demanding regime of scrutiny and must satisfy tests of necessity and proportionality.

[8] See Resta (2022), p. 323. The author points out, p. 327, that the hinge of the proposal seems to lie in the definition of a regulatory model aimed at the optimal management of the risks inherent in the use of artificial intelligence devices, with the primary objective of protecting fundamental rights and safeguarding the democratic process. Compare Imbruglia (2021), p. 157; Uricchio et al. (2020); Calzolaio (2020), p. 1; Alpini (2019), p. 1.

[9] Amendments adopted by the European Parliament on 14 June 2023 on the proposal for a regulation of the European Parliament and of the Council on laying down harmonized rules on artificial intelligence (Artificial Intelligence Act) and amending certain Union legislative acts (COM(2021)0206 – C9-0146/2021 –2021/0106(COD))1.

would not have otherwise taken in a manner››.[10] These are types of risk with a very blurred boundary compared to what is considered systemic risk for the Digital Services Act.

The Digital Services Act considers negative consequences for the physical and mental well-being of the person in general to be a systemic risk, without requiring that they be the result of subliminal techniques, although Article 34 of the Digital Services Act specifies that when conducting risk assessments, providers of very large online platforms and of very large online search engines shall analyse whether and how the systemic risk are influenced by intentional manipulation of their service, including by inauthentic use or automated exploitation of the service.

Another element to be highlighted from the comparison of the two legislative texts is that the artificial intelligence practices prohibited by the Artificial Intelligence Act concern all entities that use artificial intelligence systems and not only very large platforms. Thus, not being a large platform exempts one from the requirements of the Digital Services Act for systemic risks, but not from having to comply with the Artificial Intelligence Act when using artificial intelligence systems.

Related to this is another very interesting aspect that distinguishes the Digital Services Act from the Artificial Intelligence Act. In the Digital Services Act, in fact, there are separate obligations in proportion to the size of the digital service intermediaries. The Artificial Intelligence Act, on the other hand, provides for the same obligations regardless of the size of the company. In this respect too, therefore, there is a lack of coordination between the two measures. The consequence is that small companies will inevitably find it much more difficult to cope with the burdens of the Proposed Artificial Intelligence Act than large companies, with a further discriminatory effect on market access.[11]

5.3 Digital Services and Artificial Intelligence Systems

Digital service intermediaries are increasingly using artificial intelligence systems. These systems are constantly evolving and operate in a dynamic environment, so that the implementation of reliable artificial intelligence is an ongoing process that poses many difficulties and must be proportionate to the specific context in which

---

[10] Interesting on this point is EDPB-EDPS Joint Opinion 5/2021 on the proposal for a Regulation of the European Parliament and of the Council laying down harmonised rules on artificial intelligence. https://edpb.europa.eu. There we read that ‹‹Article 5 of the Proposal risks paying lipservice to the "values" and to the prohibition of AI systems in contrast with such values. Indeed, the criteria referred to under Article 5 to "qualify" the AI systems as prohibited limit the scope of the prohibition to such an extent that it could turn out to be meaningless in practice (e.g. "causes or is likely to cause [...] physical or psychological harm" in Article 5(1)(a) and (b)››. On this point see Orlando (2022), p. 362. The author states that the AI proposal has prohibited, in points a) and b) of Article 5, the placing on the market, commissioning and use of marketing software products capable of distorting people's behaviour, while providing for a requirement, that of the harmfulness of the product in terms of physical or psychological harm to people, which could constitute a "very high bar".

[11] Finocchiaro (2022), p. 321.

it operates and the impact it may have. Suffice it to say that an artificial intelligence application that suggests reading an unsuitable book carries far less risk than one that misdiagnoses a cancer and, therefore, cannot fail to be subject to stricter supervision.[12]

Whereas 70 of the Digital Services Act specifies that a core part of the online platform's business is the way information is prioritised and presented on its online interface to facilitate and optimise access to information for the recipients of the service. This is done, for example, by algorithmically suggesting, ranking and prioritising information, distinguishing through text or other visual representations, or otherwise curating information provided by recipients.

Systems using such algorithms cannot fail to also fall within the scope of the Artificial Intelligence Act if one only considers the very definition of an artificial intelligence system, which, in fact, also refers to a machine-based system that is designed to operate with varying levels of autonomy and that can, for explicit or implicit objectives, generate outputs such as predictions, recommendations, or decisions, that influence physical or virtual environments.[13]

If, therefore, the intermediary of digital services uses such systems, he will be the recipient of what is provided for by the Artificial Intelligence Act, independently and irrespective of other specific provisions of the Digital Services Act and also of the distinction between hosting, online search engines and online platforms or very large online platforms that underlies the different obligations outlined by the Digital Services Act.

Article 1 of the Artificial Intelligence Act, moreover, is explicit in specifying that it harmonised transparency rules for artificial intelligence systems intended to interact with natural persons, emotion recognition systems and biometric categorisation systems, and artificial intelligence systems used to generate or manipulate image, audio or video content.

It follows that, for example, the provisions of Article 52 of the Artificial Intelligence Act are applicable to intermediaries of digital services, to the extent that such intermediaries are users of an emotion recognition system or a biometric categorisation system that interacts with natural persons. These must be informed about the operation of the system.

Furthermore, again applying Article 52 of the Artificial Intelligence Act, digital service intermediaries, who are users of an artificial intelligence system that generates or manipulates text, audio or visual content that would falsely appear to be authentic or truthful and which features depictions of people appearing to say or do things they did not say or do, without their consent ('deep fake'), shall disclose in an appropriate,

[12] COM (2019) 168 final, p. 5. See Wagner (2018), p. 1; Jabłonowska et al. (2018), p. 17, where we read that «there is not one AI problem, and there will be not one solution to challenges posed by AI. On the contrary, the response will be different across the sectors, both regarding the substance and form of the potential regulatory response».

[13] See Amendment 165 of the Amendments adopted by the European Parliament on 14 June 2023 on the proposal for a regulation of the European Parliament and of the Council on laying down harmonized rules on artificial intelligence (Artificial Intelligence Act) and amending certain Union legislative acts (COM (2021)0206 – C9-0146/2021 –2021/0106(COD))1.

timely, clear and visible manner that the content has been artificially generated or manipulated, as well as, whenever possible, the name of the natural or legal person that generated or manipulated it.[14]

Another example of frequent use of algorythms by digital service intermediaries is content moderation. Providers often rely on automated search techniques and means,[15] even though they are aware that they cannot grasp the peculiarities of the context in which certain phrases are inserted, risking, for instance, blocking content that is erroneously offensive in nature.[16]

A major dilemma for operators of content detection algorithms is whether to prioritize over-removal errors, so-called false positives, or under–removal errors, so-called false negatives.

A strict content removal policy will result in a high rate of false positives, harming the freedom of expression of the person whose content was wrongly removed. A lax policy will result in a high rate of false negatives, which harms the victims of the content that should have been removed but wasn't, such as the owner of a copyright.[17]

The Digital Services Act is alert to the problems posed by moderating content by automated means. Under Article 16 of the Digital Services Act, for instance, if hosting service providers use automated means for processing any notices that they receive and making decisions, they must necessarily include information on the use of such means.

---

[14] See Amendment 486 of the Amendments adopted by the European Parliament on 14 June 2023 on the proposal for a regulation of the European Parliament and of the Council on laying down harmonized rules on artificial intelligence (Artificial Intelligence Act) and amending certain Union legislative acts (COM (2021)0206 – C9-0146/2021 –2021/0106(COD))1.

[15] Cosio (2020) p. 898. The author analyses the jurisprudence of the Court of Justice of the European Union on the basis of which it is considered that the exclusion from the general obligation of active surveillance ex ante of the content published by users, provided for by Article 15 of the E-Commerce Directive, is not contrary to the judge's order to the social network operator to remove information with content identical and/or equivalent to that of information previously declared unlawful, where two conditions are met. Surveillance and active search is limited to content, in essence, unchanged from that which gave rise to the finding of unlawfulness. The equivalent contents to be removed are identified by the judicial or administrative authority in a clear and precise manner, so that the service provider does not have to make an autonomous assessment of them, being able to resort to automated procedures.

[16] See Court of Justice of the European Union, 12 July 2011, L'Oréal v. eBay on this point of particular interest is also Commission Communication of 28 September 2017, COM (2017)555—Tackling Illegal Content Online—Towards an enhanced responsibility of online platforms. Here it is pointed out that online platforms have technical tools to identify and remove illegal content, from simple metadata filtering to calculated addressing and content tagging, so-called fingerprinting. Quarta and Smorto (2020), p. 283, state that it should not be overlooked that the provider could be exposed to the risk of actions for damages by those who requested the transmission of information that later turned out not to be harmful to the right of a third party. On this point, of particular interest is the solution of the Digital Millennium Copyright Act, which protects the provider from the risk of a claim for damages for the removal of content that does not turn out to be unlawful, but at the same time allows the removal of allegedly unlawful content even in the face of a communication from the person who claims to have been harmed. However, it will then be the reporter who will have to compensate for the damage if his allegation turns out to be unfounded.

[17] Maxwell (2022) p. 6.

Moreover, if a hosting service provider decides to remove specific information provided by service users or to disable access to it, pursuant to Article 17 of the Digital Services Act, shall provide a clear and specific statement of reasons to any affected recipients of the service at the latest at the time of the removal or disabling of access; the statement of reasons shall contain information on the use made of automated means in taking the decision, including information on whether the decision was taken in respect of content detected or identified using automated means.

Furthermore, with regard to online platforms, the Digital Services Act is explicit in prohibiting the exclusive use of automated means in the internal complaint-handling system and imposes, as one of the transparent reporting obligations for online platform providers, for the purposes of the report referred to in Article 15 of the Digital Services Act, to provide information on any use of automated means for content moderation purposes, including a description of the precise purposes, indicators of the accuracy of the automated means in pursuing those purposes, and any safeguards applied.

The explicit aim, as can be seen from Article 20 of the Digital Services Act is that providers of online platforms shall handle complaints submitted through their internal complaint-handling system in a non-discriminatory manner, under the supervision of appropriately qualified staff, and not solely based on automated means.

Article 15 of the Digital Services Act limiting itself to providing, among the obligations of transparent communication for intermediary service providers, also that relating to the measures taken to provide training and assistance to staff members engaged in content moderation.[18]

The role of moderators is very delicate because they ensure human control and they are deputed to take decisions that, since they may affect fundamental rights, should be taken by subjects, and in a manner that ensures adequate guarantees of protection.

5.4 Digital Services and Human Oversight

The awareness of the important role of human oversight emerges in Artificial Intelligence Act where it defines artificial intelligence system a software that for a given set of human-defined objectives, generate outputs such as content, predictions, recommendations, or decisions influencing the environments they interact with.[19]

The reference to human-defined objectives enhances their role against a path that had started from the idea of recognising the legal personality of these systems, precisely to mark their autonomy from humans. One only must think of the European

[18] See Franchi (2021).

[19] A definition of Artificial Intelligence is also found in the "Proposition de loi constitutionnelle relative à la Charte de l'intelligence artificielle et des algorithmes", deposited on 15 January 2020, in France, at the Assemblée Nationale. About the first attempts to define Artificial Intelligence see Marvin et al. (2006) p. 12.

Parliament Resolution of 16 February 2017 with recommendations to the Commission on Civil Law Rules on Robotics.[20] A position that the European Union has progressively abandoned.[21]

Human oversight is one of the seven key requirements that artificial intelligence applications should respect to be considered trustworthy. This is already apparent from the Comunication of the European Commission "Building Trust in Human-Centric Artificial Intelligence",[22] but it is made explicit in the European Parliament Resolution of 20 October 2020 with recommendations to the Commission on the Digital Services Act: Improving the functioning of the Single Market, where it is expressly stated that the 'human in command' principle must be respected, inter alia, to prevent the rise of health and safety risks, discrimination, undue surveillance, or abuses, or to prevent potential threats to fundamental rights and freedoms.[23] The importance of the role of human oversight is confirmed by European Parliament Resolution of 20 October 2020 with recommendations to the Commission on a framework of ethical aspects of artificial intelligence, robotics and related technologies[24] which proposes an approach to artificial intelligence whereby any artificial high–risk technologies shall be developed, deployed and used in a manner that guarantees full human oversight at any time. Such technologies shall be developed, deployed and used in a manner that allows full human control to be regained when needed, including through the altering or halting of those technologies.

The Artificial Intelligence Act is explicit in recognising a central role for human oversight.[25] In fact, for some high-risk artificial intelligence systems, even the involvement of a single human being is insufficient, requiring that ‹‹no action or decision is taken by the user based on the identification resulting from the system unless this has been verified and confirmed by at least two natural persons››.[26]

Measures related to human oversight are among those that must be disclosed in order to ensure the transparency of artificial intelligence systems.[27] This is what

---

[20] For a critique of the European Parliament Resolution of 16 February 2017, see Passagnoli (2019), p. 79. On this point compare Perlingieri (2015) p. 1235; Busto (2017), p. 499; Oriti (2017); Di Rosa (2022), p. 163; Astone (2022), p. 29.

[21] Orlando (2022), p. 355, notes that the suggestion of considering artificial intelligence systems as embodied entities is completely inconsistent with the legal framework and the precise choices of legislative technique made in the Artificial Intelligence Act.

[22] In COM (2019) 168 final are identify seven key requirements that artificial intelligence applications should respect to be considered trustworthy. The seven key requirements are: Human agency and oversight; Technical robustness and safety; Privacy and data governance; Transparency; Diversity, non-discrimination and fairness; Societal and environmental well-being; Accountability.

[23] Point 41) of the European Parliament Resolution of 20 October 2020 with recommendations to the Commission on the Digital Services Act: Improving the functioning of the Single Market. https://www.europarl.europa.eu

[24] https://www.europarl.europa.eu.

[25] Davis (2020), p. 304, believes that human beings may have an ongoing role to play in supervising artificial intelligence from ethical and legal perspectives, despite impressive technological advances.

[26] Article 14 of the Artificial Intelligence Act is detailed in its references to human oversight.

[27] Rotenberg (2022), p. 153, shows that the goal of algorithmic transparency is to ensure accuracy and fairness in decisions concerning individuals. Artificial intelligence techniques replicate bias,

emerges from Article 13 of the Artificial Intelligence Act, which is of particular interest because of the reference to the need for the outputs of artificial intelligence systems to be interpreted and for users to be provided with all the necessary information to facilitate such interpretation.[28]

Human oversight is seen in both the Digital Services Act and the Artificial Intelligence Act as a means of risk management and mitigation, also with explicit reference to non-discrimination.[29]

References

Achleitner RA (2022) Der digital services act als risikobasierte regulierung—Zu den Auswirkungen des risikobasierten ansatzes des DSA auf desinformation und den grundrechtsschutz. MR–Int 4:114–121

Alpini A (2019) Sull'approccio umano–centrico all'intelligenza artificiale. Riflessioni a margine del "Progetto europeo di orientamenti etici per una IA affidabile." Comparazione e diritto civile 2:1–9

Astone F (2022) Artificial Intelligence: ipotesi per una regolazione normativa. In: Cuocci V, Lops FP, Motti C (eds) Atti della summer school 2021. Cacucci, Bari, pp 29–44

Benedetti AM (2021) Contratto, algoritmi e diritto civile transnazionale: cinque questioni e due scenari. Rivista di diritto civile 3:411–426

Busto N (2017) La personalità elettronica dei robot: logiche di gestione del rischio tra trasparenza e fiducia. Ciberspazio e diritto: rivista internazionale di informatica giuridica 18:499–511

Calzolaio E (2020) Introduzione. In: Calzolaio E (ed) La decisione nel prima dell'intelligenza artificiale. Wolters Kluwer-Cedam, Milan, pp 1–5

Davis J (2020) AI, ethics, and law: a way forward. https://doi.org/10.2139/ssrn.3711040. Accessed 19 June 2023

Di Rosa G (2022) Soggettività giuridica e responsabilità robotica, in La responsabilità civile nell'era digitale. In: Cuocci V, Lops FP, Motti C (eds) Atti della summer school 2021. Cacucci, Bari, pp 163–180

Finocchiaro G (2022) La proposta di regolamento sull'intelligenza artificiale: il modello europeo basato sulla gestione del rischio. Diritto dell'informazione e dell'informatica 2:303–322

Franchi J (2021) Gli obsoleti. Il lavoro impossibile dei moderatori di contenuti. Agenzia X, Milan

Giorgini E (2019) Algorithms and law. Ital Law J 5:131–149

Herbosch M (2022) The diligent use of ai systems: a risk worth taking? J Eur Consum Mark Law 11:14–22

Imbruglia D (2021) Note sulla regolazione della IA. In: Orlando S, Capaldo G (eds) Annuario 2021. Osservatorio giuridico sulla innovazione digitale. University Press, Rome

Jabłonowska A, Kuziemski M, Nowak AM, Micklitz HW, Pałka P, Sartor G (2018) Consumer law and artificial intelligence: challenges to the EU consumer law and policy stemming from the business' use of artificial intelligence: final report of the ARTSY project. EUI Law 11:1–70

---

and as these techniques become more complex, bias becomes more difficult to detect. But the principle of algorithmic transparency remains important across a wide range of sectors.

[28] On the need for algorithmic decisions to be interpreted see Giorgini (2019) p. 145.

[29] See Artificial Intelligence Act, where it is stated that the proposal complements existing Union law on non-discrimination with specific requirements that aim to minimise the risk of algorithmic discrimination, in particular in relation to the design and the quality of data sets used for the development of artificial intelligence systems complemented with obligations for testing, risk management, documentation and human oversight throughout the artificial intelligence systems' lifecycle.

Marvin J, Minsky L, Rochester N, Shannon CE (2006) A proposal for the dartmouth summer research project on artificial intelligence, August 31, 1955. AI Mag 27:12–15

Maxwell W (2022) Applying Net neutrality rules to social media content moderation systems. Annales des Mines—Enjeux Numérique 1:90–98

Neuwirth RJ (2023) The EU artificial intelligence act: regulating subliminal AI systems. Routledge, London

Oriti S (2017) Brevi note sulla risoluzione del Parlamento europeo del 16 febbraio 2017 concernente le norme di diritto civile sulla robotica. https://www.ratioiuris.it/brevi-note-sulla-risoluzione-del-parlamentoeuropeo-del-16-febbraio-2017-concernente-le-norme-diritto-civile-sulla-robotica. Accessed 19 July 2023

Orlando S (2022) Regole di immissione sul mercato e «pratiche di intelligenza artificiale» vietate nella proposta di Artificial Intelligence Act. Persona e Mercato 3:346–367

Passagnoli G (2019) Ragionamento giuridico e tutele nell'intelligenza artificiale. Persona e Mercato 3:79–85

Perlingieri C (2015) L'incidenza dell'utilizzazione della tecnologia robotica nei rapporti civilistici. Rassegna di diritto civile 4:1235–1246

Quarta A, Smorto G (eds) (2020) Diritto privato dei mercati digitali. Le Monnier University, Milan

Cosio R (2020) La responsabilità del prestatore di servizi di hosting. Jus Civile 4:887–905

Resta G (2022) Cosa c'è di "europeo" nella Proposta di Regolamento UE sull'intelligenza artificiale? Diritto dell'informazione e dell'informatica 2:322–342

Rotenberg M (2022) Artificial intelligence and the right to algorithmic transparency. In: Ienca, Pollicino O, Liguori L, Stefanini E, Andorno R (eds) The cambridge handbook of information technology, life sciences and human rights. Cambridge University Press, Cambridge, pp 153–165

Smuha NA, Ahmed–Rengers E, Harkens A, Li W, MacLaren J, Piselli R, Yeung K (2021) How the EU can achieve legally trustworthy AI: a response to the European Commission's Proposal for an Artificial Intelligence Act. https://doi.org/10.2139/ssrn.3899991

Tommasi S (2023) Digital Services Act e Artificial Intelligence Act: tentativi di futuro da armonizzare. Persona e Mercato 2:279–296

Uricchio AF, Riccio G, Ruffolo U (eds) (2020) Intelligenza Artificiale tra etica e diritti. Prime riflessioni a seguito del libro bianco dell'Unione europea. Cacucci, Bari

Wagner B (2018) Ethics as an escape from regulation: from ethics–washing to ethics–shopping? In: Bayamlioglu E, Baraliuc I, Janssens LAW, Hildebrandt M (eds) Being profiled: cogitas ergo sum: cogitas ergo sum: 10 years of profiling the European Citizen. Amsterdam University Press, Amsterdam, pp 84–89

Chapter 6
Towards the Future: Risk as Opportunity

Abstract The comparison between the Digital Services Act and the Artificial Intelligence Act shows under what conditions the risk-based approach can be an opportunity for the future. The importance of attention to risk, even in facing the challenges that artificial intelligence systems bring, cannot be separated from an awareness of the limits of law. Law may intervene to prevent damage, but before knowing whether the damage will actually occur or when the damage has already occurred and therefore there is no risk. The limits of law in the face of risk must not lead to an excessive reliance on ethics. It is not only the distinction between different types of risks that should be the central aspect. Rather, it is necessary to also have a critical attitude towards the tendency to humanise artificial intelligence systems.

Keywords Risk · Future · Ethics · AI Liability

6.1 Limits of Law in the Face of Risk and the Over-Reliance on Ethics

The importance of attention to risk, even in facing the challenges that artificial intelligence systems bring, cannot be separated from an awareness of the limits of law in the face of risk.[1]

In fact, law may intervene either before the action, preventing it from being carried out, but before knowing whether the eventuality of the harm would have occurred, or when the event has already occurred and, therefore, there is no longer a risk.[2]

[1] See De Giorgi (2018), p. 12; Nuzzo (2018), p. 261, states that Hegel's thought also assumes the philosophical centrality of the limit. And with Kant and beyond Kant, the limit is thought of as relation. The limit, then, is not a thing, but the being in relation to the thing. It is the other of both things that it helps to define. For a reflection on the history of risk see Alabrese (2009).

[2] The most serious problem that the legal system faces is the difficulty of accepting its riskiness and controlling its temporal instability through recourse to the function traditionally performed by normativity, that is, by validity: to provide the certainty that there will be a right in any case. The certainty, that is, that whatever the outcome of the conflict, whatever the expectation or whatever the resistance or disappointment, there will still be a right. In these terms De Giorgi (2015), p. 77.

S. Tommasi, *The Risk of Discrimination in the Digital Market*,
SpringerBriefs in Law, https://doi.org/10.1007/978-3-031-43640-6_6

Risk is a strategy for imputing future harm to a decision.[3] Thus, what can be done is not to avoid the risk, but to channel its harmful consequences. Channelling the harmful consequences of risk means monetarising it and turning it into an economic risk, through, for example, insurance mechanisms.[4] This is a solution to which a great increase in risk can certainly be linked. He who is insured against risk is inclined to engage in risky behaviour precisely because, should the risk occur, he feels secure. This behaviour, however, is experienced as a danger to others.[5]

In addition, there is currently a great deal of uncertainty as to how the liability rules apply in the case of the use of artificial intelligence systems.[6] This results in difficulties in assessing concrete liability exposures and, consequently, in having the relevant insurance cover.[7] It is particularly difficult in artificial intelligence systems to

---

[3] De Giorgi (2015), p. 399; Petrocco (2018) p. 690; Faini (2018), p. 638.

[4] Who has been harmed may have less chance of obtaining effective redress and higher costs to enforce their rights than in situations where the harm is caused by traditional technologies. This allows one to understand the importance given by COM (2019) 168 final to the accountability of artificial intelligence systems, which refers to a proactive attitude towards a future action, on which one must then be able to report once it has occurred. Accountability is a way of reassuring potential users that, regardless of the outcome of costly error research, they will get compensation. Comandé (2018), p. 1012, argues that accountability can have a procedural and a substantive meaning and that in the first case, it indicates a kind of procedural regularity that guarantees everyone that the same procedure is applied equally to everyone and is not designed in such a way as to disadvantage one group or subject in a specific way. In substantive terms, accountability requires that the policy choice made promotes fundamental objectives or principles.

[5] See De Giorgi (2015), p. 64. The author gives the example of the doctor who is insured and is less concerned about any negative consequences of his diagnosis than is a doctor who does not have his own insurance. The patient experiences the risk of error as a danger from which he cannot escape and against which he cannot take any action until the damage has occurred. On the relationship. between liability for risk and insurability of it to determine ex ante who must prepare to suffer the risk in Trimarchi (1961) p. 31. As to the relationship. between the cause of covering the risk and the insurance cause, see Corrias (2006), p. 263. Recently, also for a bibiographic reconstruction about the relationship. between alea and risk, see Caggiola (2022).

[6] See Zuddas (2020), p. 424. The author warns that the management of the risk of algorithmic discrimination could be entrusted to the distinction between the principle of prevention and the precautionary principle. The distance between the two principles depends on the nature of the risk. The precautionary principle is applied in the presence of unknown risks, which take on the character of a threat, since it is not possible to determine either the magnitude or the time at which the harmful event might occur. The precautionary principle is a response to the inconveniences arising from scientific uncertainty. The precautionary principle, on the other hand, is applied in the presence of known risks, which take on the character of a danger, referable to harmful events attested by scientific evidence. The precautionary principle can be applied both in the algorithm processing phase and in the phase of selecting data to be entered into the computer system. The precautionary principle, on the other hand, finds an ideal place of application in the imposition of limits on the autonomous and, to some extent, uncontrolled operation of machine learning systems.

[7] Chamberlain (2023), p. 12, asks: ‹‹with the consumer collective paying more for the product or service, insurance is included. How will these insurance policies work, considering that the object of insurance is widely unknown?››. The author states that even though this appears to be a relevant question from a tort law point of view, the concept of ensuring the unknown is no novelty within the insurance industry, where the entire idea of insuring risks builds on fictive scenarios. In fact, it

allocate obligations among the economic actors involved,[8] and it is often impossible to trace the sources of data used by an algorithm, since data may be provided by several parties or other artificial intelligence devices.[9]

It is no coincidence that liability issues are the most significant obstacle for companies wishing to adopt artificial intelligence systems and that they must adopt appropriate conformity assessments and post–market monitoring mechanisms. This clearly emerges from the articulated process that seems to affect attempts to regulate civil liability regime for artificial intelligence. Suffice it to say that COM (2022) 496 of 29 September 2022, Proposal for a Directive of the European Parliament and of the Council on adapting non–contractual civil liability rules to artificial intelligence known as Artificial Intelligence Liability Directive,[10] which shares little with the previous European Parliament Resolution of 20 October 2020 with recommendations to the Commission on a civil liability regime for artificial intelligence.[11]

The Artificial Intelligence Liability Directive opts for the harmonisation of existing national fault–based liability regimes,[12] unlike the European Parliament's Resolution of 20 October 2020 on a civil liability regime for artificial intelligence, which introduced the notions of back–end and front-end operator and provided for strict liability.

In particular, in high-risk artificial intelligence systems, the choice was in the direction of strict liability of the operator of the artificial intelligence system,[13] who would only be exempt from liability for damage or harm due to force majeure. In artificial intelligence systems that could not be defined as high-risk, the choice was in the direction of a presumption of fault on the part of the operator. In the Artificial Intelligence Liability Directive, instead, it is left to the future to assess whether strict liability regimes and forms of insurance coverage should be introduced.

---

can be assumed that risks and liability connected to artificial intelligence are already regulated in a variety of insurance clauses around the world.

[8] See Jacobs and Simon (2022), p. 6. The authors emphasise that most artificial intelligence systems are complex socio-technical systems in which control over the system is extensively distributed. Therefore, determining sensible addressees for the respective obligations is all but trivial.

[9] See Mökander et al. (2021), p. 12. The authors are also referred to for an exemplification. They state that «for example, consider the requirement that high-risk artificial intelligence systems shall be designed with capabilities to automatically record (or 'log') their operations and decisions (Proposed Artificial Intelligence Act, Article 12). These logs can either be controlled by the user, the provider, or a third party, as per contractual agreements. In any case, however, it is the provider's responsibility to ensure that, and plan for how, high-risk artificial intelligence systems automatically generate logs».

[10] www.eur-lex.europa.eu.

[11] www.eur-lex.europa.eu. See Garreffa (2020) p. 502; Albanese (2023) p. 439.

[12] De Mari Casareto Dal Verme (2022), p. 500.

[13] On the different allocation of risks in cases of liability for fault and strict liability, see Trimarchi (1961) p. 13, where, with reference to the development of industrial activities, it is noted that the exercise of such activities necessarily entails a series of unavoidable accidents, despite the use of the utmost diligence and, given the complexity of the organisation, fault is divided, in correspondence with the division of labour, into a thousand small negligible portions, each insufficient to justify the liability of its author. See also Trimarchi (2021), p. 75.

The limits of law in the face of risk must not lead to an excessive reliance on ethicsintended, as is the case in the documents concerning AI, as self-regulation.[14]

Formulas of marked rhetorical value such as "human-centric" or "trustworthy-AI" reflect the idea that artificial intelligence applications can affect the system of protection of human dignity and fundamental rights, so that a pure model of self-regulation is inappropriate.[15]

It has been pointed out that, on the one hand, self–regulation is commendable. It can hardly be denied that ethical artificial intelligence is preferable over unethical AI. Self-regulation could help mitigate discrimination and could provide inspiration for legislators. On the other hand, there are serious problems with self-regulation. Most importantly: self–regulation is non-binding. Human rights protection cannot be left to voluntary measures.[16]

Excessive reliance on self-regulation causes a tendency to overlook certain risks. Consider the so-called "ethics washing". Many artificial intelligence self–regulatory principles are rather vague, do not provide detailed guidelines and may distract legislators from their efforts to improve standards and prevent companies from seeing ethics as the "easy" or "soft" option.[17]

No less relevant are the risks from digital ethics shopping and digital ethics lobbying. The latter is identified as the "malpractice of ex–ploiting digital ethics

---

[14] See Floridi (2022, 2021, 2019).

[15] Resta (2022), p. 327. The author considers that it is only through a hard-law approach that an acceptable balance between the protection of the individual and other competing interests, such as innovative experimentation and economic growth, can be achieved. See Pascuzzi (2020), p. 307.

[16] Floridi (2019) p. 188. Particularly confident in an ethical approach to the problems posed by artificial intelligence systems is Katyal (2019), p. 56. In particular, the author explores the impending conflict between the protection of civil rights and artificial intelligence. While both areas of law have amassed rich and well-developed areas of scholarly work and doctrinal support, a growing body of scholars are interrogating the intersection between them. The author ‹‹argues that the issues surrounding algorithmic accountability demonstrate a deeper, more structural tension within a new generation of disputes regarding law and technology». See Van Berkel et al. (2023), p. 2.

[17] Wagner (2018), p.1, says that a strange confusion among technology policy makers can be witnessed at present. While almost all can agree on the common chorus of voices chanting 'something must be done,' it is very difficult to identify what exactly must be done and how. In this confused environment it is perhaps unsurprising that the idea of 'ethics' is presented as a concrete policy option. Striving for ethics and ethical decision-making it is argued, will make technologies better. While this may be true in many cases, much of the debate about ethics seems increasingly focussed on private companies avoiding regulation. Unable or unwilling to properly provide regulatory solutions, ethics is seen as the 'easy' or 'soft' option which can helpstructure and give meaning to existing self-regulatory initiatives. In this world, 'ethics' is the new "industry self-regulation". Hasenbein (2020) focuses on the question of ethical guidelines in times of digitalisation and artificial intelligence. It also examines the role of humans during these developments and what distinguishes them from machines and robots. Compare Galimberti (2020, 2022), p. 219. The author states that ethics as a form of acting in view of ends celebrates its impotence in the world of technology, regulated by doing as pure production of results. This means that it is no longer ethics that chooses the ends and instructs technology to find the means, but it is technology that, by taking the results of its procedures as ends, conditions ethics by forcing it to take a position on a reality that is no longer natural but artificial.

to delay, revise, replace, or avoid good and necessary legislation (or its enforcement) about the design, development, and deployment of digital processes, products, services, or other solutions".[18] Digital ethics shopping, on the other hand, refers to the circumstance that one ends up with a large number of principles, codes, guidelines or ethical frameworks, producing a proliferation of documents that generate inconsistency and confusion. Moreover, public and private actors often design their own codes for fear of appearing inferior to others, thus further contributing to information redundancy. In other words, there is a risk that all this hyperactivity ends up being a way of justifying one's own behaviour, rather than making it consistent with a shared ethical framework.[19]

Through the screen of presenting a solution as ethical, more serious and increasingly difficult problems can be generalised. Awareness of this, if it cannot avoid the malpractices discussed above, can help reduce their negative effects, which are even more insidious the more they are concealed by the noble reference to ethics.[20]

The risks associated with the use of artificial intelligence systems must not be concealed by the "inflation of moral communication".[21] One cannot think of protecting social systems from themselves by institutionalising the ethical control of their operating codes. Recourse to ethics is highly inflated because the illusion is cultivated that ethics allows for decision-making rules that can be rationally grounded and practicable. Morality cannot have the function "of immunising individual social systems—a specific function which is fulfilled by law and which it would be tragic if it were possible to take away from law and return once again to morality".[22]

---

[18] Floridi (2019), p. 188.

[19] Floridi (2019), p. 188. Digital ethics dumping and ethics shirking are also recurrent in contexts of disadvantaged populations, weaker institutions, legal uncertainties and corrupt regimes. The first one is understood as a «malpractice of (a) exporting research activities about digital processes, products, services, or other solutions, in other contexts or places (e.g. by European organisations outside the EU) in ways that would be ethically unacceptable in the context or place of origin and (b) importing the outcomes of such unethical research activities». Ethics shirking is understood as «malpractice of doing increasingly less Bethical work (suchas fulfilling duties, respecting rights, and honouring commitments) in a given context the lower the return of such ethical work in that context is mistakenly perceived to be.

[20] Smuha et al. (2021), p. 1, focus on the concept of "Lawful AI", pointing out that it was mentioned but not developed in the Commission's High-Level Expert Group. On AI's Ethics Guidelines for Trustworthy AI (2019), which instead confined its discussion to the concepts of "Ethical" and "Robust" AI. Detailed recommendations for the Proposal's revision are also discussed there.

[21] De Giorgi (2015), p. 144.

[22] De Giorgi (2015), p.145. The author recalls that Luhmann already stated in 1989 that this ethics has the function of a utopia in the precise and paradoxical sense of Thomas More's Utopia. It indicates topos that cannot be found, a place that does not exist. Under the name of ethics, society procures the possibility of introducing the negation of the system into the system and to speak in an honourable manner. The fact that it is this ethics of the counter-devo (Gegensoll- Ethik, in his words) is proof of the autonomy and operational closure of the system, which can deal (umzugehen) even with the negation of the system in the system. The author emphasises, p. 143, that when the operating codes of individual social systems are attacked or contaminated, morality is resorted to, but it does not solve the problem because to moralise does not mean to apply moral norms that allow one to formulate a decision, or that allow one to evaluate a fact. Morality is not a set of norms

The ethical aspects of artificial intelligence are at the heart of the aforementioned European Parliament resolution of 20 October 2020 with recommendations to the Commission on a framework of ethical aspects of artificial intelligence, robotics and related technologies, which, in addition to Article 5,entitled Ethical Principles of Artificial Intelligence,[23] is of interest here because it provides, under Article 16, for a European Certificate of Ethical Compliance issued by a Supervisory Authority, if full human control, at all times, of artificial intelligence technologies and the absence of distortions and discrimination are guaranteed.

6.2 Limits of the Tendency to Humanise Artificial Intelligence Systems

The adjectivizations of risk, moreover, not accompanied by a uniform and clear definition of what is meant by risk, end up leaving knots unresolved and relying too much on the construction of a complex bureaucratic framework forced to work on blurred distinctions.

Therefore, it is not only the adjectivization of risk and the distinction between different types of risks that should be the central aspect of an attempt to legally regulate digital servants that increasingly make use of artificial intelligence systems. Rather, it is necessary to have also a critical attitude towards attempts to apply to artificial intelligence systems the semantics used for humans and to construct the rationality of the future by looking at old requirements for stabilising expectations that no longer operate.[24] From the perspective of renouncing the application to artificial intelligence systems of the semantics used for humans, artificial intelligence must not evoke functions comparable to those of the human brain.[25]

---

that must be applied. Morality is the set of conditions that are fixed in social communication as the conditions of the attribution of consideration or contempt of the other, so that he acts as an individual.

[23] Article 5 of the European Parliament Resolution of 20 October 2020 with recommendations to the Commission on a framework of ethical aspects of artificial intelligence, robotics and related technologies states that any artificial intelligence, robotics and related technologies, including software, algorithms and data used or produced by such technologies, shall be developed, deployed and used in the Union in accordance with Union law and in full respect of human dignity, autonomy and safety and other fundamental rights set out in the Charter. Any processing of personal data carried out in the development, deployment and use of artificial intelligence, robotics and related technologies, including personal data derived from non-personal data and biometric data, shall be carried out in accordance with Regulation (EU) 2016/679 and Directive 2002/58/EC. The Union and its Member States shall encourage research projects intended to provide solutions, based on artificial intelligence, robotics and related technologies, that seek to promote social inclusion, democracy, plurality, solidarity, fairness, equality and cooperation.

[24] In the studies on mind, machines and artificial intelligence, reference is obligatory to Turing (1950), p. 433. On Turing's thought see Giunti and Giuntini (2007), p. 39.

[25] Giuffrida et al. (2018), p. 750. The authors say ‹‹words like "language", "memory", "understand", "instruction", "read", "write", "command", and many others are in constant use. They are words

On these aspects, explicit indications can be drawn also from the "Avis relatif à l'impact de l'intelligence artificielle sur les droits fondamentaux", of the "Commission nationale consultative des droits de l'homme (CNCDH)". In the Plenary Assemblyé of 7 April 2022, the CNCDH states that indeed an excess of anthropomorphisation in the terms used, starting with that of "artificial intelligence", but also when it comes to "neural networks", "deep learning". This leads to confusion about what is meant by "artificial intelligence". This leads to confusion about the real possibilities offered by data processing systems, which are based on procedures coded in computer systems: it is above all a question of mathematics. All actors, both in the public and private sectors, should therefore avoid using this expression because of its psychological impact, which can lead to reticence or, on the contrary, to exaggerated confidence and acceptance. This is why the CNCDH recommends that public institutions and the media favour more neutral expressions, such as "algorithmic decision support systems".

The limits of a vision that tends to humanise artificial intelligence systems can be well exemplified by the experiment proposed by Searle.[26] He imagines being enclosed in a room that communicates with the outside only through a slit. Outside the room there are Chinese gentlemen who write questions, in Chinese, on some sheets of paper and then pass these sheets to Searle through the slit. Searle is a native English speaker and knows absolutely no Chinese, indeed, he cannot even recognise that the signs on the sheets he receives are ideograms of that language. However, inside the room, Searle has a large and detailed book, written in English, which tells him, solely through descriptions of the shape of the signs, which other signs he must write in response. Having received a sheet of paper, Searle then consults the rule book, writes the answer following the book's instructions and passes it outside to the Chinese gentlemen. The gentlemen outside, understanding Chinese, understand the answers written by Searle, and since these answers make complete sense, they are certain that there is someone in the room who, like them, can understand Chinese. Instead, we know that Searle does not know that language at all and is therefore completely unable to understand either the meaning of the signs he receives or those he produces himself. Moreover, the mere formal manipulations that Searle makes following the rules of the book will never even enable him to learn the meaning of

---

which, in their primary meaning, have reference to cognitive beings. Computers are not cognitive››. In discussing artificial intelligence as the ability of a machine to intelligently imitate human behaviour, one can refer to aforementioned European Parliament's Resolution of 20 October 2020 on a civil liability regime for artificial intelligence, where it is proposed to use the term "automated decision-making" rather than Artificial Intelligence, precisely to avoid the ambiguities of the latter expression. Automated decision-making involves a user delegating initially a decision, partly or completely, to an entity by way of using software or a service; that entity then in turn uses automatically executed decision-making models to perform an action on behalf of a user, or to inform the user's decisions in performing an action.

[26] See Searle (1980) p. 417. The anthropocentric approach to artificial intelligence may be reductive if it is conditioned by the tendency to "humanise machines" from the point of view of language, concepts and related issues, and if it focuses on artificial intelligence as an instrument serving only the human person. Compare Calzolaio (2020), p. 1; Alpini (2019); Tommasi (2020), p. 853.

those signs. The general conclusion Searle draws is that semantics or intentionality cannot be the product of a mere execution of formal rules.

The way in which both Searle and the digital computer produce such responses is essentially the same because both do nothing more than execute formal rules (the instructions in the book for Searle, those in the programme for the digital computer). But then, if semantics or intentionality cannot be the product of a mere execution of formal rules, the digital computer, which does nothing else, will lack such attributes.[27] Instead, however, thought and intelligence cannot be devoid of semantics or intentionality.[28]

Artificial intelligence systems can do things that humans cannot, but conversely, algorithms do not have a human dimension, but are means.[29]

Even if we admit that with reference to algorithms we can speak of "electronic agents actors", we would have to agree that this is "another subjectivity" with respect to the human one. We would have to agree that this is "another subjectivity" with respect to human subjectivity, and that we are therefore dealing with "rational actors" but "in no way human".[30]

---

[27] Giunti, Giuntini (2007), p. 6.

[28] Searle (1980), p. 417, says that ‹‹(1) intentionality in human beings (and animals) is a product of causal features of the brain. I assume this is an empirical fact about the actual causal relations between mental processes and brains. It says simply that certain brain processes are sufficient for intentionality. (2) Instantiating a computer program is never by itself a sufficient condition of intentionality››. From these premises, the author draws the following conclusions: consequences: the explanation of how the brain produces intentionality cannot be that it does it by instantiating a computer program. Any mechanism capable of producing intentionality must have causal powers equal to those of the brain. Any attempt literally to create intentionality artificially (strong AI) could not succeed just by designing programs but would have to duplicate the causal powers of the human brain.

[29] On this point, see De Giorgi and Luhmann (2013), p. 27. On the circumstance of non-humans being able to communicate with humans see Latour (2004), p. 71. In this perspective, such communication can take place in different ways. The simplest is the one in which the algorithm is only a tool that humans make use of, but there can also be a kind of interoperability between man and machine, such that we can speak of a hybrid. On this point compare Teubner (2019), (2006), p. 521, The author compares the thinking of Luhmann with that of Latour and says «however impressive this theoretical move appears, it does not go far enough to cover the far-reaching ambitions of the ecological movement and the cyber revolution. Collectives, i.e. social systems between human individuals, as actors - this is the point where Luhmann stops and where Latour begins. In Latour's account, a multitude of new actants and hybrids that cannot be identified with human individuals or with collective actors, are entering the scene and radically transforming today's political ecology». The author also says that «regarding both Luhmann and Latour: Personification of nonhumans is best understood as a strategy of dealing with the uncertainty about the identity of the other, which moves the attribution scheme from causation to double contingency and opens the space for presupposing the others' selfreferentiality. Beyond Luhmann: There is no compelling reason to restrict the attribution of action exclusively to humans and to social systems. Personifying other nonhumans is a social reality today and a political necessity for the future. Beyond Latour: The admission of actors does not take place, as he suggests, into one and only one collective. Rather, the properties of new actors differ extremely according to the multiplicity of different sites of the political ecology».

[30] See Teubner (2006), p. 500; More generally on the distinction between the problems of the human person from the problems of any other centre of subjective imputation compare Perlingieri (2020a),

At least as things stand at present, one cannot speak of artificial surrogates of the person or their volitions.[31] Artificial intelligence does not dispose of genuinely subjective acts, but makes calculations and reproduces attitudes, and must not pose as a "free pass" to avoid the kinds of control that can instead be demanded of human beings. Demanding explanations from artificial intelligence systems is reasonable, and that we should start by asking of our artificial intelligence systems what we ask of humans.[32]

It is reductive, therefore, to anthropologise digital processes, as we have tried to demonstrate by favouring the angle of observation of the right not to be discriminated against, and on closer inspection, it is also reductive to consider artificial intelligence as a tool only at the service of people or human beings, and not also of the environment and all the living beings that populate it.[33]

This is borne out by the fact that to obtain a reliable artificial intelligence, its impact on other sentient beings must also be considered, who must be able to benefit from biodiversity and a habitable environment,under the banner of sustainable technological progress that is attentive to the ecosystem, in a logic of coexistence between part (man) and whole (ecological system).[34]

6.3 Risk as Opportunity

The limits of the tendency to humanise artificial intelligence systems, also from a perspective of protection against discrimination in the digital marketplace, highlight the need to ensure that, in some way, the human possibility to influence the operation and output of artificial intelligence tools is safeguarded. There is further confirmation of the importance of human oversight.[35]

The human possibility of influencing the operation and output of artificial intelligence tools, at least by activating oversight tools, is of particular interest, because it is what makes automated decision–making tools risky in the positive sense.

What has been said can be clear if one considers the distinction between risk and danger.[36]

---

p. 101; Perlingieri (2020b), p. 257; Perlingieri (1972); Falzea (1939) p. 54; Alcaro (1976); Femia (2019), p. 9; Portaluri (2019) p. 5; Míguez Núñez (2019).

[31] Criticise the tendency to anthropomorphise the phenomenon and narrate it as if the artificial intelligences involved were emanations of human subjects: Finocchiaro (2018), p. 441; Sartor (2002), p. 465; Pardolesi and Davola (2020) p. 108.

[32] Doshi-Velez et al. (2017).

[33] On the urgent need to set the relationship between man and nature on a new footing with a view to ecological balance, compare Grisi (2020), p. 190; Larrère and Larrère (2018), p. 338; Khakurel et al. (2018), p. 13.

[34] Monteduro and Tommasi (2015) p. 167; Capobianco (2023), p. 651.

[35] Tommasi (2022), p. 67.

[36] On the difference between risk and danger see Luhmann (1991); De Giorgi (1994), p. 45.

Risk is a constraint of the future that makes it possible to act under the conditions of not knowing under which choices are made in the present. Risk is not thought of as a datum or a subterranean reality that runs hidden beneath action, nor as the opposite of security, i.e. "an artificial condition of stability and certainty that is assumed to be rational".[37]

Risk, in other words, is not a reality but the possibility of a harmful event that another decision could have avoided. If I do not have a choice, it is not a risk, so that if it is inevitable that harm will occur, I am not faced with a risk but with a danger.

Risk, then, should not be seen as the breakdown of an order that would otherwise continue to exist, but rather as a way through which social systems adapt to the complexity of their environment, and modern society is a risk society in the sense that it has created conditions that allow it to construct different futures, to keep the contingency of events high, i.e. to keep more and more possibilities open and, when, as a result of a decision, damage occurs that one would have wanted to avoid, to know that another decision could have avoided it.[38]

The alternative to risk, therefore, is not security but danger.

If all forms of control of the decision–making mechanism and all kinds of human intervention are excluded, then there is no possibility of human participation in the decision and, therefore, there is danger and not risk. If all forms of control of artificial intelligence systems and all kinds of human intervention are excluded, then there is a situation that cannot be controlled and, therefore, is worse than a situation that, being risky, is controllable.

What makes artificial intelligence system risky is the possibility of a form of human involvement with respect to the operation and output produced by an artificial intelligence system.

In other words, artificial intelligence systems are risky insofar as they allow decisions not to be entrusted exclusively to the machine, but also to those evaluations that are the preserve of humans alone.[39] If there is no human input, we must be aware that we expose ourselves to uncontrollable dangers.

The certainly not insignificant role given to human oversight highlights the limits of an approach based on the necessary opacity of algorithmic decision-making processes. If opacity were to preclude any kind of human intervention in artificial intelligence systems, it would be a danger, not a risk.

If spaces for human control were to be maintained, as, inter alia, required by the above-mentioned regulation, the opacity of algorithmic decision-making can be considered to be a specific risk relating to artificial intelligence systems.[40] In view of

---

[37] De Giorgi (2015), p. 61.

[38] De Giorgi (2015), p. 62.

[39] See Andorno (2022), p. 273. The paper is of particular interest in the part where it examines two different meanings of human dignity: the classical one that refers to the intrinsic value of everyone, and the more recent one that refers to the integrity and identity of the human race, including future generations.

[40] Burrell (2016), p. 1, distinguishes between the various forms of algorithmic opacity. The author draws a distinction between three forms of opacity: (1) opacity as intentional corporate or state secrecy, (2) opacity as technical illiteracy, and (3) an opacity that arises from the characteristics of

this risk, the European Commission considers it necessary to provide for transparency requirements for algorithms, which are also particularly important for the ex–post mechanism for monitoring compliance with the regulation and for strengthening trust in the use of these means.[41] To this end, it is crucial, on the one hand, that artificial intelligence systems are identifiable as such, so that users know they are interacting with an artificial intelligence system, and, on the other, that humans can understand how the system has made algorithmic decisions, even if they do not need to understand every single step of the decision-making process.[42]

Jurisprudence has highlighted the practical importance of such assumptions. In Italy, in a case concerning some teachers affected by a procedure of recruitment and assignment to school seats that was entrusted to an algorithm whose functioning it was not possible to know, the Council of State[43] affirmed that the knowability of the algorithm must be guaranteed in all aspects and must allow for the verification that the criteria, assumptions and outcomes of the algorithmic procedure conform to the prescriptions and purposes established by law. In particular, it has been pointed out that the multidisciplinary characterisation of the algorithm does not exempt the need for the "technical formula", which in fact represents the algorithm, to be accompanied by explanations that translate it into the underlying "legal rule" and make it readable and comprehensible.

This is not an isolated case. In France, the use of the Parcoursup platform designed by both the French Ministry of Education and the French Ministry of Higher Education, Research and Innovation has received much attention.

The Parcoursup platform is intended for high school students, apprentices or students in reorientation who wish to enroll in public higher education. The platform

machine learning algorithms and the scale required to apply them usefully. The author argues that recognizing the distinct forms of opacity that may be coming into play in each application is a key to determining which of a variety of technical and non-technical solutions could help to prevent harm.

[41] The importance of algorithmic transparency can also be deduced from the so-called "duty of explanation" of the Guidelines for Trustworthy Artificial Intelligence of 8 April 2019, where reference is made to the aim of making not only the decision-making criteria of algorithmic agents based on artificial intelligence understandable, but also their aims and objectives. On this aspect see Zuiderveen Borgesius (2020), p. 9, where we read that «even when assuming that people have a right to explanation regarding algorithmic decisions, it is often difficult, if not impossible, to explain the logic behind a decision, when an algorithmic system arrives at that decision after analysing large amounts of data. Moreover, in some circumstances, an explanation might not be of much help to people». On this point compare Alpa (2020); Alpa (2019); Longo and Scorza (2020); Santosuosso (2020); Ruffolo (2020); Gabrielli and Ruffolo (2019), p. 1657.

[42] Pajno et al. (2019), p. 13.

[43] Italian Council of State, 4 February 2020, No. 881, point 10. Explicit in this direction is also the Italian Civil Cassation, 25 May 2021, no. 14380, which clarified, in the case of a web platform designed to process the reputational profiles of individuals, that the requirement of awareness of the consent to the processing of personal data cannot be considered satisfied where the algorithm's implementation scheme and the elements of which it is composed remain unknown or cannot be known by the data subjects.

allows the future student to learn about the different courses and institutions that interest him, to formulate wishes and validate the admission proposals received.[44]

The French Constitutional Council, decision of 3 April 2020 stipulated that third parties, and not only the addressees of decisions, can access the criteria used by the algorithm to enable them to identify possible biases. General published information on algorithmic processing on the one hand, and individual explanations of a given decision on the other, must in any case be provided to the public and users in an accessible and intelligible language. Information for professionals involved in algorithmic processes, both employees and public servants, must enable them to understand the general functioning of the tool, to develop their vigilance regarding the risks of bias and to ensure their effective control of the processing.[45]

It is therefore necessary to pay attention not only to the risks associated with artificial intelligence systems, but also to how to use these systems without exposing ourselves to uncontrollable dangers and to uncontrollable infringements of rights, such as the right not to be discriminated against.

From this point of view, reflection on risk and the distinction with danger is fundamental in building a sustainable future. Where sustainability is understood not only as safeguarding the environment but also as safeguarding the rights of the individual also in the digital sphere.[46]

References

Alabrese M (2009) Riflessioni sul tema del rischio nel diritto agrario. ETS, Pisa

Albanese A (2023) Mobilità del futuro e funzione preventiva della responsabilità civile. Europa e diritto privato 2: 439-450

Alcaro F (1976) Riflessioni critiche intorno alla soggettività giuridica. Significato di un'evoluzione. Giuffrè, Milan

Alpa G (2019) Fintech: un laboratorio per i giuristi. Contratto e impresa 2:377–385

Alpa G (2020) (ed) Diritto e intelligenza artificiale. Pacini Giuridica, Pisa

Alpini A (2019) Sull'approccio umano–centrico all'intelligenza artificiale. Riflessioni a margine del "Progetto europeo di orientamenti etici per una IA affidabile." Comparazione e diritto civile 2:1–9

Andorno R (2022) Human dignity, life sciences technologies and the renewed imperative to preserve human freedom. In: Ienca M, Pollicino O, Liguori L, Stefanini E, Andorno R (eds) The

[44] https://www.service-public.fr/particuliers/vosdroits/R42572?lang=en.

[45] Decision 3 April 2020, No. 2020-834 QPC. See also Decision 8 April 2019 No. 2019-099 concerning the operation of the Parcoursup platform; Council of State 12 June 2019 No. 427916. The attention of the French legal system to the importance of transparency of artificial intelligence systems also emerges from the Code des relations entre le public et l'administration (CRPA). See Papin (2020); Bourcier and De Filippi (2018).

[46] On the need for an analysis based on the principle of sustainability, compare Fracchia (2010), p. 41; Iannarelli (2015); p. 13; Pennasilico (2015), p. 40; Landini (2015), p. 611; Caterini (2018), p. 39; Perlingieri (2020a, b), p. 101; Capriglione (2022), p. 25.; De Franceschi (2022) p. 236; De Franceschi (2023), p. 45.

Cambridge Handbook of Information Technology, Life Sciences and human rights. Cambridge University Press, Cambridge, pp 273–285
Bourcier D, De Filippi P (2018) La transparence des algorithmes face à l'Open Data: Quel statut pour les données d'apprentissage? Revue française d'administration publique. https://hal.science/hal-01850926/document. Accessed 20 May 2023
Burrell J (2016) How the machine 'Thinks': Understanding opacity in machine learning algorithms. Big Data Soc 6:1–12
Caggiola N (2022) I contratti di gioco e scommessa. Percorsi evolutivi dal codice civile alla disciplina consumeristica. Giappichelli, Turin
Calzolaio E (2020) Introduzione. In: Calzolaio E (ed) La decisione nel prima dell'intelligenza artificiale. Wolters Kluwer-Cedam, Milan, pp 1–5
Capobianco E (2023) The New Deal for Consumers. Jus Civile 3:651–660
Capriglione F (2022) Responsabilità sociale di impresa e sviluppo sostenibile. Rivista trimestrale di diritto dell'economia 4:1–25
Caterini E (2018) Sostenibilità e ordinamento civile. Per una riproposizione della questione sociale. ESI, Naples
Chamberlain J (2023) The risk-based approach of the European Union's proposed artificial intelligence regulation: some comments from a tort law perspective. Eur J Risk Regul 14:1–13
Comandé G (2018) Responsabilità ed accountability nell'era dell'Intelligenza Artificiale. In: Di Ciommo F, Troiano O (eds) Giurisprudenza e autorità indipendenti nell'epoca del diritto liquido. Studi in onore di Roberto Pardolesi. La Tribuna, Piacenza, pp 1001–1014
Corrias P (2006) Garanzia pura e contratti di rischio. Giuffrè, Milan
De Franceschi A (2022) The digitalization of contract law facing the sustainability challenge: the italian experience towards the development of EU Law. J Eur Consum Mark Law 11:236–248
De Franceschi A (2023) The sustainability of consumer and market law: green claims, greenwashing and the right to repair. J Eur Consum Mark Law 12:45–48
De Giorgi R (1994) O risco na sociedade contemporânea. Seqüência Estudos Jurídicos e Políticos 15: 45–54
De Giorgi R (2005) Il Diritto nella società del rischio. Revista Opinião Jurídica 5:395–407
De Giorgi R, Luhmann N (2013) [1991] Teoria della società. Franco Angeli, Milan
De Giorgi R (2015) Temi di filosofia del diritto. Pensa MultiMedia, Lecce
De Giorgi R (2018) Presentazione. In: De Giorgi R (ed), Limiti del diritto. Prospettive di riflessione e analisi. Pensa MultiMedia, Lecce, pp 11–18
De Mari Casareto Dal Verme T (2022) Verso la AI Liability Directive: la proposta della Commissione europea del 28 settembre 2022 per una direttiva sull'adattamento delle regole di responsabilità civile all'Intelligenza Artificiale. Persona e Mercato. Osservatorio OGID 2:500–502
Doshi–Velez F, Kortz M, Budish R, Bavitz C, Gershman S, O'brien D, Scott K,. Shieber S, Waldo J, Weinberger D, Weller A, Wood A (2017) Accountability of AI Under the Law: The Role of Explanation. https://doi.org/10.48550/arXiv.1711.01134
Faini F (2018) Dati, informazione e società digitale: il cambiamento nei confini del diritto. In: De Giorgi R (ed) Limiti del diritto. Prospettive di riflessione e analisi. Pensa MultiMedia, Lecce, pp 638–646
Falzea A (1939) Il soggetto nel sistema dei fenomeni giuridici. Giuffrè, Milan
Femia P (2019) Il civile senso dell'autonomia. The Cardozo Electronic Law Bulletin 25:1–11
Finocchiaro G (2018) Il contratto nell'era dell'intelligenza artificiale. Rivista trimestrale di diritto e procedura civile 2:441–460
Floridi L (ed) (2021) Ethics, governance, and policies in artificial intelligence. Springer, Berlin
Floridi L (2022) Etica dell'intelligenza artificiale. Raffaello Cortina Editore, Milan
Floridi L (2019) Translating principles into practices of digital ethics: five risks of being unethical. Philosophy & Technology 32:185–192
Fracchia F (2010) Sviluppo sostenibile e diritti delle generazioni future. Rivista quadrimestrale di diritto dell'ambiente 0:13–41

Gabrielli E, Ruffolo U (2019) (ed) Intelligenza Artificiale e diritto. Giurisprudenza italiana (numero monografico) 7:1657–1778

Galimberti U (2022) I miti del nostro tempo. Feltrinelli, Milan

Galimberti U (2020) Heidegger e il nuovo inizio. Il pensiero al tramonto dell'Occidente. Feltrinelli, Milan

Garreffa S (2020) La risoluzione del Parlamento europeo del 20 ottobre 2020 sul regime di responsabilità civile per l'intelligenza artificiale Persona e Mercato. Osservatorio OGID 4:502–504

Giuffrida I, Lederer F, Vermerys N (2018) A legal perspective on the trials and tribulations of AI: how artificial intelligence, the internet of things, smart contracts, and other technologies will affect the law. Case W Res Law Rev 68:747–781

Giunti M, Giuntini R (2007) Macchine, calcolo e pensiero. In: Ancini S (ed) Sguardi sulla scienza nel giardino dei pensieri. Mimesis Edizioni, Milan, pp 1–21

Grisi (2020) La lezione del Coronavirus. Jus Civile 1:190–214

Hasenbein M (2020) Ethik in Zeiten von Digitalisierung und künstlicher Intelligenz. In: Der Mensch im Fokus der digitalen Arbeitswelt. Springer, Berlin, pp 185–200

Iannarelli A (2015) Cibo e diritti. Per un'agricoltura sostenibile. Giappichelli, Turin

Jacobs M, Simon J (2022) Assigning obligations in AI regulation: a discussion of two frameworks proposed by the European commission. https://doi.org/10.1007/s44206-022-00009-z

Katyal SK (2019) Private accountability in the age of artificial intelligence. UCLA Law Rev 66:54–141

Khakurel J, Penzenstadler B, Porras J, Knutas A, Zhang W (2018) The Rise of Artificial Intelligence under the Lens of Sustainability. Technologies 6:1–18

Landini S (2015) Clausole di sostenibilità nei contratti tra privati. Problemi e riflessioni. Diritto pubblico 2:611–636

Larrère C, Larrère R (2018) Penser et agir avec la nature. Une enquête philosophique. La Découverte, Paris

Latour B (2004) Politics of nature: how to bring the sciences into democracy. Harvard University Press, Cambridge

Longo A, Scorza G (2020) Intelligenza artificiale. L'impatto sulle nostre vite, diritti e libertà. Mondadori, Milan

Luhmann N (1991) Soziologie des Risikos. De Gruyter, Berlin

Míguez Núñez R (2019) Le avventure del soggetto. Contributo teorico–comparativo sulle nuove forme di soggettività giuridica. Mimesis Edizioni, Milan–Udine

Mökander J, Axente M, Casolari F, Floridi L (2021) Conformity assessments and post–market monitoring: a guide to the role of auditing in the proposed European AI regulation. Mind Mach 32:241–268

Nuzzo L (2018) Riflessioni sui limiti del diritto. Jacques Derrida, Niklas Luhmann e la differenza del diritto. In: De Giorgi R (ed), Limiti del diritto. Prospettive di riflessione e analisi. Pensa MultiMedia, Lecce, pp 255–265

Pajno A, Bassini M, De Gregorio G, Macchia M, Patti FP, Pollicino O, Quattrocolo S, Simeoli D, Sirena P (2019) AI: profili giuridici. Intelligenza Artificiale: criticità emergenti e sfide per il giurista. BioDiritto 3:205–235

Papin E (2020) Dans l'enfer du droit d'accès aux algorithmes de l'administration. http://www.feral-avocats.com/fr/publication/dans-lenfer-du-droit-dacces-aux-algorithmes-de-ladministration. Accessed 19 Juli 2023

Pardolesi R, Davola A (2020) Algorithmic legal decision making: la fine del mondo (del diritto) o il paese delle meraviglie? Questione Giustizia 1:104–111

Pascuzzi G (2020) Il diritto dell'era digitale. Il Mulino, Bologna

Pennasilico M (2015) Sviluppo sostenibile, legalità costituzionale e analisi "ecologica" del contratto. Persona e Mercato 2:37–50

Perlingieri G (2020a) «Sostenibilità», ordinamento giuridico e «retorica dei diritti». A margine di un recente libro. Foro Napoletano 1:101–118

Perlingieri P (1972) La personalità umana nell'ordinamento giuridico. ESI, Naples
Perlingieri P (2020b) Il diritto civile nella legalità costituzionale secondo il sistema italo-europeo delle fonti. I. Metodi e tecniche. ESI, Naples
Petrocco G (2018) Lentezza del diritto (limite) e velocità della rete (illimitato). Una lettura della modernità a partire dalle pagine del Filebo. In: De Giorgi R (ed) Limiti del diritto. Prospettive di riflessione e analisi. Pensa MultiMedia, Lecce, pp 629–637
Portaluri PL (2019) L'articolazione delle figure soggettive: dalla personalità alla soggettività giuridica. https://ridiam.it/wp-content/uploads/2019/06/05-07-8.-Larticolazione-delle-figure-soggettive-dalla-personalit%C3%A0-giuridica-alla-soggettivit%C3%A0-giuridica-Portaluri.pdf. Accessed 10 June 2023
Resta G (2022) Cosa c'è di "europeo" nella Proposta di Regolamento UE sull'intelligenza artificiale? Diritto dell'informazione e dell'informatica 2(322):342
Ruffolo U (ed) (2020) Intelligenza Artificiale. Il diritto, i diritti, l'etica. Giuffrè, Milan
Santosuosso A (2020) Intelligenza artificiale e diritto. Perché le tecnologie di IA sono una grande opportunità per il diritto. Mondadori, Milan
Sartor G (2003) Gli agenti software: nuovi soggetti del ciberdiritto? Contratto e impresa 3:55–87
Searle JR (1980) Minds, brains and programs. Behav Brain Sci 3:417–457
Smuha NA, Ahmed–Rengers E, Harkens A, Li W, MacLaren J, Piselli R, Yeung K (2021) How the EU can achieve legally trustworthy AI: a response to the European Commission's proposal for an Artificial Intelligence Act. https://doi.org/10.2139/ssrn.3899991
Teubner G (2006) Rights of non–humans? Electronic agents and animals as new actors in politics and law. J Law Soc 33:497–521
Teubner G (2019) Soggetti giuridici digitali? Sullo status privatistico degli agenti software autonomi. Femia P (ed). ESI, Naples
Tommasi S (2020) L'intelligenza artificiale antropocentrica: limiti e opportunità. Jus Civile 4:853–886
Tommasi S, Monteduro M (2015) Paradigmi giuridici di realizzazione del benessere umano in sistemi ecologici ad esistenza indisponibile e ad appartenenza necessaria. In: Benessere e regole dei rapporti civili. Lo sviluppo oltre la crisi. ESI, Naples, pp 161–202
Tommasi S (2022) Intelligenza artificiale: il rischio come opportunità. Revista do Tribunal Regional Federal da 1ª Região 34:67–74
Trimarchi P (1961) Rischio e responsabilità oggettiva. Giuffrè, Milan
Trimarchi P (2021) La Responsabilità Civile: Atti Illeciti, Rischio, Danno. Giuffrè, Milan
Turing AL (1950) Computing machinery and intelligence. Mind 49:433–460
Van Berkel N, Sarsenbayeva Z, Goncalves J (2023) The methodology of studying fairness perceptions in artificial intelligence: contrasting CHI and FAccT. Int J Hum Comput Stud 170:1–25
Wagner B (2018) Ethics as an escape from regulation: from ethics–washing to ethics–shopping? In: Bayamlioglu E, Baraliuc I, Janssens LAW, Hildebrandt M (eds) Being profiled: cogitas ergo sum. 10 years of profiling the European Citizen. Amsterdam University Press, Amsterdam, pp 84–89
Zuddas P (2020) Intelligenza Artificiale e Discriminazioni. Consulta Online 2:408–425
Zuiderveen Borgesius FJ (2020) Strengthening legal protection against discrimination by algorithms and artificial intelligence. Int J Human Rights 24:1–22

Chapter 7
Perspectives and Conclusions

Abstract A reasonable digital transformation is possible if we do not neglect the potentially discriminatory scope of the activities of digital service providers, who are increasingly using artificial intelligence tools. It is therefore necessary to consider not only the human limitations but also of those of artificial intelligence systems, which cannot be entrusted with rights that are indispensable for sustainable development. Human oversight means that one does not necessarily have to be subjected to the automated decision. In this sense, human oversight is what makes automated decision–making processes risky in the positive sense. Risk, in fact, is an opportunity because it allows one to choose between different futures. Danger is something uncontrollable to which one is exposed without any possibility of influence.

Keywords Digital transformation · Human oversight · Artificial intelligence systems · Sustainable development

The new technologies impact on our world, challenging man's sense of uniqueness and forcing him to review his relationship with himself[1] and to confront the "fourth narcissistic wound".[2]

---

[1] This is the thought of Floridi (2020). We are in the fourth revolution, that of information and communication technologies. Copernicus removed the Earth from the centre of the universe; Darwin deprived homo sapiens of his privileged position in the world of the living; Freud and, more recently, neuroscience have challenged the subject's presumed sovereignty over his own inner life, as man is dominated by the unconscious. Today, information and communication technologies contribute to a further decentralisation of man. We are not isolated and unique entities, but rather organisms, whose substratum is informational (inforgs), mutually connected and part of an environment made up of information (infosphere), which we share with natural or artificial agents, like us. On this point, see Federico (2022), p. 533; Femia (2019) p. 9. The author states that discourses are now anonymous matrices. Law can do without men, like economics, it calculates lives like any other entity. On discourses as anonymous matrices, see Teubner (2006), p. 16. Compare Hensel and Teubner (2006).

[2] Abriani and Schneider (2021), p. 300.

S. Tommasi, *The Risk of Discrimination in the Digital Market*,
SpringerBriefs in Law, https://doi.org/10.1007/978-3-031-43640-6_7

Before it was man who moulded the system in which he was embedded in his own image,[3] now we have built a system that in turn reconstructs us in its own image and that records, archives and uses, even to our detriment, all the online activity we do.[4]

At the same time, technological development is not only unstoppable, but stimulated by individual states and the European Union, which suffers, on this front, from strong competition from the United States,[5] China[6] and Japan.[7] It is no coincidence that we speak of empires of artificial intelligence and the economic, political and social forces that shape it.

Faced with this scenario, the path towards the future must consider that not only the human being has limits, but also digital business, especially when it makes use of artificial intelligence tools.

Even the digital age has, in fact, its sins, seven as tradition dictates, and which have been enumerated as follows: inequality; commercial exploitation and information abuse; privacy risks; disintegration of communities; instant plebiscites and dissolution of democracy; tyranny of those who control access; loss of value of public service and social responsibility.[8]

Expectations of a space without limits and boundaries and without intermediation have been frustrated, with inevitable repercussions on expectations of greater inclusion and protection of differences. These, in fact, have also been frustrated, while we are witnessing increasingly invasive and insidious forms of domination over our present.

The analysis of the potentially discriminatory scope of the digital market also provides a practical demonstration of the ambivalent nature of technological development which, while on the one hand creates new opportunities, on the other hand introduces new risks.[9]

---

[3] See Brown (1994) p. 32; Frosini, p. 95, in which one wonders in particular about the influences of the cybernetic dimension on social behaviour.

[4] On the circumstance that we have renounced (or have allowed ourselves to be forced to renounce) to consider ourselves (or nations or classes or humanity) as the subjects of history; we have dethroned ourselves and in our place, we have placed other subjects of history, indeed only one other subject: technology—On its course, on its use, depends the being or non-being of humanity. In these terms Anders (1992), p. 258.

[5] See the National AI Initiative Act of 2020, part of the National Defense Authorization Act of 2021 and National AI Initiative Office; United States Innovation and Competition Act of 2021. www.congress.gov. See also Artificial Intelligence Capabilities and Transparency (AICT) Act and the Artificial Intelligence for the Military (AIM) Act, both part of the FY 2022 National Defence Authorisation Act.

[6] Tian and Li (2022), p. 9; Hao Yang (2022), p. 12; Chai (2022).

[7] On the European aspiration to export a model that is not only regulatory, but cultural, see Finocchiaro (2022), p. 303, where the so-called Brussels Effect is also discussed. On this point compare Bendiek and Stuerzer (2023), p. 1.

[8] This is the doctrine of Rodotà (1997) p. 31.

[9] As for the fact that the digital revolution implies doubts and concerns, but also extraordinary opportunities, see Floridi (2022), p. 297. The author believes that the digital revolution has only just begun, and, because of this, we have the chance to shape it in a positive sense, to the benefit of

Among the risks that can arise in the digital environment, the risk of discrimination was chosen to be analysed. The European Union is aware of this risk, as demonstrated most recently both in the European Declaration on Digital Rights and Principles for the Digital Decade and in the European Parliament Resolution of 13 December 2022 on the Digital Divide: the social differences created by digitalisation.

But this is also confirmed by the timely regulation of the Digital Services Act and the Digital Markets Act. The latter only indirectly concerns end–users and addresses the problems of possible discrimination in terms of access and permanence in the digital market for business users. The Digital Services Act, on the other hand, concerns end–users directly, aiming to protect them from discrimination they may suffer either as individuals, as members of vulnerable groups or as members of society.

The European Union, in the Digital Services Act, has sought a solution in terms of protection from the risk of discrimination by equating discriminatory content with illegal content, relying on stricter notice and takedown mechanisms and greater liability for providers. The latter, in particular, are the recipients of obligations and responsibilities proportional to the degree of risk introduced into the system.

Regarding the protection of non–discrimination, these are important steps forward, since the right not to be discriminated against can be violated not only by a denial of access to digital services or by the unjustifiable removal of content that one would like to disseminate, but also by the failure to provide adequate mechanisms to combat illegal content.

Various articles of the Digital Services Act show that there are few cases in which digital service providers can be considered mere transmitters of other people's content.

Suffice it to think, for instance, of Article 14 of the Digital Services Act in the part in which it provides not only that providers of intermediary services shall include information on any restrictions that they impose in relation to the use of their service, but also that providers of intermediary services must apply and enforce such restrictions in a diligent, objective and proportionate manner. Whereas 26 of the Digital Services Act states that the condition of acting in good faith and in a diligent manner should include acting in a non–discriminatory manner.

Non–discriminatory acting therefore plays a strategic role in the Digital Services Act because it is indicative of diligent acting. In identifying forms of protection against the risk of discrimination in the digital market, however, the Digital Services Act cannot be taken as the sole point of reference.

Providers of digital services, in fact, increasingly use artificial intelligence systems. The right to non–discrimination, the possible infringement of which is considered a systemic risk by the Digital Services Act, is affected by the increasing

humanity and the planet. Using a metaphor, the author, p. 336 et seq, to highlight the uniqueness of the human being states that humans are a beautiful mistake in the great software of the universe. On the perfection of nature and the ability of science to identify the mathematical laws that govern it, see Amendola (2022).

use of algorithms. The examples of algorithmic discrimination in the digital market are now many.

The potential discriminatory scope of artificial intelligence systems in the intermediation of digital services highlights, with reference to protection from the risk of discrimination in the digital market, the limits of European anti–discrimination legislation and the need for multilevel protection, also entrusted to the rules governing artificial intelligence systems.[10]

Regarding the limits of European anti–discrimination legislation in tackling the problems that arise in the digital market, it should be observed that European legislation is too closely linked to lists and typical causes of discrimination and is not suited to adequately counteracting discrimination linked to formally neutral characters, but which recur frequently in protected categories. The examples given on advertising, recommendation systems and dynamic pricing highlighted this fact, which is even more worthy of attention if one considers that, unfortunately, algorithms are often presented and perceived as neutral tools.

Complicating the picture, in terms of non–discrimination protection, is the speed and ontological immediacy of the digital world, amplified using artificial intelligence systems. These characteristics are difficult to reconcile with the prudence and depth required for decisions that impact on people's rights and lives.

Digital services and artificial intelligence systems are not, therefore, worlds apart, but, on the contrary, often, enevitably, connected. It is no coincidence, moreover, that both the Digital Services Act and the Artificial Intelligence Act adopt a risk–based approach that, while on the one hand makes it possible to avoid excessive restrictions, on the other hand is not without some criticalities.[11] Consider the fact that risk is linked to the probability of occurrence of events that are considered negative. In this perspective, however, emphasis is placed on problems specific to statistics and not to risk, yet statistics concern the past, whereas risk is projected into the future. Probability presupposes a comparison and comparison makes sense, even in statistics, between comparable data. The point is that data concerning the generality cannot be compared with data concerning the individual, claiming, for example, that what is not risky for others must also be felt by the individual as not risky.

The individual is not a probability and risk are not a measure.

There is also a lack of a clear definition of risk and, what is more, new types of risk are introduced which, although they play a central role in regulatory terms, are not always clearly identifiable.[12] One thinks, for example, of systemic risk in

---

[10] Bernitz et al. (2020).

[11] Chamberlain (2023), p. 3. The author points out that the European approach is based on general risk regulation, but that rules for specific legal sectors are also necessary. It is also emphasised that the Artificial Intelligence Act starts with prohibitions and not with what is permitted, contrary to other important European regulations such as the GDPR.

[12] See EDPB-EDPS Joint Opinion 5/2021 on the proposal for a Regulation of the European Parliament and of the Council laying down harmonised rules on artificial intelligence, cit. p. 2, where it is stated that EDPB and the EDPS welcome the risk-based approach underpinning the Proposal. However, this approach should be clarified and the concept of "risk to fundamental rights" aligned

the Digital Services Act and of unacceptable risk in the Artificial Intelligence Act, where reference is also made to high risk and low or minimal risk.

We are faced with a legal framework that is very punctual, but not always harmonised and consistent and still too little concerned with remedial profiles. This is evidenced by the comparison between the Digital Services Act and the Artificial Intelligence Act from which it emerged that digital service providers, insofar as they can be considered users of artificial intelligence systems, are subject to the provisions of the Artificial Intelligence Act regardless of the distinction between hosting, online search engines and online or very large online platforms.

For instance, regardless of the provisions of the Digital Services Act, digital service providers cannot use an artificial intelligence system that generates risks unacceptable to the Artificial Intelligence Act. If digital service providers were allowed to use such artificial intelligence systems, because they are not prohibited by the Digital Services Act, it would have the effect that what is unacceptable under the Artificial Intelligence Act, is acceptable under the Digital Services Act.

Faced with this scenario, protection from the risk of discrimination in the digital market can only be entrusted to the coordination of various regulations that have a general and transversal value with respect to the directly regulated areas. Inevitable is, in fact, the reference also to the GDPR because data represent the nutriment of artificial intelligence systems. The latter feeds, however, also on non–personal data, so that the GDPR also lends itself to being an important, but not exclusive, regulatory point of reference in protecting against the risk of discrimination in the digital market.

A strategic role, albeit limited to relations between businesses and consumers, must also be acknowledged to the discipline on unfair commercial practices,[13] which can cover the spaces left empty by the GDPR with particular reference to non–personal data and to decisions that are not fully automated.

One only needs to consider that digital service intermediaries are increasingly using artificial intelligence systems that are clearly capable of influencing consumers' economic decisions.

Discriminatory advertising and dynamic prices are significant examples of the technologically organised influence on consumer choices.[14]

Therefore, the scope of the discipline on unfair commercial practices, which has not yet been exploited to its full potential, should also be exploited in the digital sphere.

Attention to the potential discriminatory scope of artificial intelligence systems in the intermediation of digital services is also important because it is an example of the contradictory nature of the exaggerated tendency to rely on anthropomorphic machines.[15] This tendency represents, in fact, the culmination of anthropocentrism,

with the GDPR and the Regulation (EU) 2018/1725 (EUDPR), since aspects related to the protection of personal data come into play.

[13] Narciso (2019), p. 147.

[14] Orlando (2022).

[15] Starting from the risks of discrimination generated using algorithms, reflection has been initiated on the fundamental rights that can be challenged by AI. This is also highlighted recently

not only legal, but philosophical and ontological in general,[16] and, at the same time, the end of the centrality of man as a unique and inimitable being, so that man's vulnerability to technological evolution becomes apparent.

On the path towards the future, we must overcome the naive contraposition between man and machine, at least for two reasons. The first: what we call artificial intelligence is a set of statistical techniques that also depend on human labour, communicate errors and network biased worldviews.[17] The second: the algorithm collects and feeds on human data, i.e. data that, more or less consciously, is shared by users in the digital marketplace.

The output is not enough; it must be contextualised and interpreted.

Hence, the still necessarily strategic role of human oversight, given the brain functions that make humans different from any artificial intelligence and other sentient creatures.[18]

Human oversight means that one does not necessarily have to be subjected to the automated decision but can in some way choose whether and how to influence that decision. In this sense, human oversight is what makes automated decision–making processes risky in the positive sense.

Risk, in fact, is an opportunity because it allows one to choose between different futures. Danger is something uncontrollable to which one is exposed without any possibility of influence. Risky artificial intelligence systems are acceptable, but not dangerous, even more so if it is only rights such as the right not to be discriminated against that are endangered. This is a danger that intermediation in digital services can make more pernicious and more pervasive. Just think of the audience reach of platforms and the automation of discrimination. The latter is even more dangerous the more it goes hand in hand with the ideological homogeneity that can be achieved if one regards our humanity as a limitation and not as a value.

References

Abriani N, Schneider G (2021) Diritto delle imprese e intelligenza artificiale. Dalla Fintech alla Corptech. Il Mulino, Bologna

Amendola L (2022) L'algoritmo del mondo: l'irragionevole armonia dell'universo. Il Mulino, Bologna

by the Commission nationale consultative des droits de l'homme and the Défenseur des droits of the French Republic, in collaboration with the Commission nationale de l'informatique et des libertés. See Report of the Défenseur des droits en partenariat avec la CNIL, Algorithmes: prévenir l'automatisation des discriminations, Dimanche 31 Mai 2020. https://www.defenseurdesdroits.fr.

[16] See Gatt (2022), p. 16. Compare Cristianini (2023).

[17] Broussard (2019), p. 7.

[18] Sadin (2019); Tomassini (2020), states that we are facing a real evolutionary leap that knows no geographical, political or ideological boundaries and that for the first time in human history involves the entire planet. The author wonders if we will be up to it, and he believes we will, thanks to our ability to resist, risk, innovate and imagine the future, actions that are exquisitely human in which no computer or artificial intelligence will ever be able to replace us.

Anders G (1992) L'uomo è antiquato. II. Sulla distruzione della vita nell'epoca della terza rivoluzione industriale. Bollati Boringhieri, Turin
Bendiek A, Stuerzer I (2023) The Brussels effect, European regulatory power and political capital: evidence for mutually reinforcing internal and external dimensions of the Brussels effect from the European digital policy debate. Digital Soc 25:1–25. https://doi.org/10.1007/s44206-022-00031-1
Bernitz U, Groussot X, Paju J, de Vries S (eds) (2020) General Principles of EU Law and the EU Digital Order. Wolters Kluwer, Alphen aan den Rijn
Broussard M (2019) Artificial unintelligence. How computers misunderstand the world. MIT Press, Cambridge
Brown L (1994) The seven deadly sins of the digital age. InterMedia 22:32–37
Chamberlain J (2023) The risk-based approach of the European Union's Proposed Artificial Intelligence Regulation: some comments from a tort law perspective. Eur J Risk Regul 14:1–13
Cristianini N (2023) La scorciatoia. Come le macchine sono diventate intelligenti senza pensare in modo umano. Il Mulino, Bologna
Federico A (2022) Il nomos della 'infosfera.' Rassegna di diritto civile 2:533–554
Femia P (2019) Il civile senso dell'autonomia. The Cardozo Electronic Law Bulletin 25:1–11
Finocchiaro G (2022) La proposta di regolamento sull'intelligenza artificiale: il modello europeo basato sulla gestione del rischio. Diritto dell'informazione e dell'informatica 2:303–322
Floridi L (2020), Pensare l'infosfera. La filosofia come design concettuale. Raffaello Cortina Editore, Milan
Floridi L (2022) Etica dell'intelligenza artificiale. Raffaello Cortina Editore, Milan
Frosini V (1968) Cibernetica. Diritto e società. Edizioni di Comunità, Milan
Gatt L (2022) Legal anthropocentrism between nature and technology: the new vulnerability of human beings. Eur J Privacy Law Technol 1:15–26
Hao Yang A (2022) Taiwan prepari lo scuso di silicio. Limes 12:125–131
Hensel I, Teubner G (2014) Matrix Reloaded Kritik der staatszentrierten Drittwirkung der Grundrechte am Beispiel des Publication Bias. https://www.jura.uni-frankfurt.de/49069887/KJ_Teubner_Hensel.pdf. Accessed 20 Juli 2023
Narciso M (2019) The regulation of online reviews in European consumer law. Eur Rev Private Law 27:557–581
Orlando S (2022) Regole di immissione sul mercato e «pratiche di intelligenza artificiale» vietate nella proposta di Artificial Intelligence Act. Persona e Mercato 3:346–367
Rodotà S (1997) Tecnopolitica. La democrazia e le nuove tecnologie della comunicazione. Laterza, Rome–Bari
Sadin E (2019) Critica della ragione artificiale. Una difesa dell'umanità. Luiss University Press, Rome
Teubner G (2006) Die anonyme Matrix. Zu Menschenrechtsverletzungen durch "private" transnationale Akteure. Der Staat: Zeitschrift für Staatslehre und Verfassungsgeschichte, deutsches und europäisches öffentliches Recht 44:161–187
Tian H, Ji Y (2022) La Cina sconfiggerà gli USA con l'intelligenza (artificiale). Limes 12:9–16